PR
6007
.E36
Z87
1988

Sternlicht, Sanford V.

R. F. Delderfield

R. F. Delderfield

Twayne's English Authors Series

Kinley E. Roby, Editor

Northeastern University

TEAS 463

R. F. DELDERFIELD
(1912–1972)
Photograph by Mark Gerson

R. F. Delderfield

By Sanford Sternlicht

Syracuse University

Twayne Publishers
A Division of G. K. Hall & Co. · Boston

R. F. Delderfield
Sanford Sternlicht

Copyright 1988 by G.K. Hall & Co.
All rights reserved.
Published by Twayne Publishers
A Division of G.K. Hall & Co.
70 Lincoln Street
Boston, Massachusetts 02111

Copyediting supervised by Lewis DeSimone
Book production by Janet Zietowski
Book design by Barbara Anderson

Typeset in 11 pt. Garamond
by R/TSI Typographic Company, Inc.
Hamden, Connecticut

Printed on permanent/durable acid-free paper
and bound in the United States of America

Library of Congress Cataloging-in-Publication Data

Sternlicht, Sanford.
    R.F. Delderfield.

    (Twayne's English authors series; TEAS 463)
    Bibliography: p.
    Includes index.
    1. Delderfield, R.F. (Ronald Frederick),
1912–1972—Criticism and interpretation.   I. Title.
II. Series.
PR6007.E36Z87   1988   823'.912   87-34975
ISBN 0-8057-6967-6 (alk. paper)

Remembering Mom and Dad
Sister Edith, Brother Jack

Contents

About the Author

Sanford Sternlicht, professor emeritus of theatre and English at the State University of New York at Oswego, now teaches in the English Department of Syracuse University. A wide-range scholar-writer-director, Professor Sternlicht is the author of the following books: *Gull's Way* (1961), poetry; *Love in Pompeii* (1967), poetry; *The Black Devil of the Bayous* (1970), history with E. M. Jameson; *John Webster's Imagery and the Webster Canon* (1972), literary criticism; *McKinley's Bulldog: The Battleship Oregon* (1977), history; *John Masefield* (Twayne's English Authors Series, 1977); *C. S. Forester* (Twayne's English Authors Series, 1981); *U.S.F. Constellation: Yankee Racehorse* (1981),history with E. M. Jameson; *Padraic Colum* (Twayne's English Authors Series, 1985); and *John Galsworthy* (Twayne's English Authors Series, 1987). He has edited *Selected Short Stories of Padraic Colum* (1985) and *Selected Plays of Padraic Colum* (1986). His many articles on subjects from Shakespeare to Graham Greene have appeared in numerous journals, including *Renaissance Papers, Papers on Language and Literature, Minnesota Review, Harvard Magazine, Florida Review, College English, Ball State Forum, Midwest Quarterly, Calcutta Review, Studies in Humanities,* and *Writers Digest.* His poetry has appeared in over three hundred publications, including the *New York Times*, the *New York Herald Tribune, Christian Science Monitor, Saturday Evening Post, Canadian Forum, Dalhousie Review,* and *Poetry Review* (London).

In 1960 Sternlicht received the *Writer Magazine* New Poets Award. In 1965 he received a poetry fellowship from the Poetry Society of America. The State University of New York Research Foundation has awarded him numerous fellowships and grants. He was Leverhulme Visiting Fellow at the University of York, England, 1965–66.

Preface

R. F. Delderfield is one of the most widely read British novelists of the twentieth century. Given the international distribution of critically acclaimed television productions of *To Serve Them All My Days, Diana*, and *A Horseman Riding By*, Delderfield may be the best-known British novelist of the post–World War II generation. His work is addictive. Readers start on a saga like *A Horseman Riding By*, in this critic's view his finest and most typical work, and find themselves on a two-thousand-page roller coaster which they are unwilling and unable to get off until the emotional ride is over. Not surprisingly, many imitators have sprung up, but to no avail. Delderfield's leisurely but always engrossing style (as with the roller coaster the speed is more apparent than real) and his impeccable social history are, in combination, as difficult to imitate successfully as Ian Fleming's James Bond adventures or C. S. Forester's Hornblower novels.

Reader response to a Delderfield saga depends to a great extent on nationality. British readers place their own pre-1970 experience or those of their parents or grandparents into the picture and become part of the panorama: one of the neighbors, or a fellow witness to the historical event, or a member of the next squadron or company in the line of battle. Sometimes the reader enters into participation with the thought: my grandmother or my grandfather did this then, was there when. Non-British readers respond more to the familial verities, the harmonization of their own idealization of generational evolution with Delderfield portraiture.

R. F. Delderfield began his writing career as a journalist, and after years of struggle he became a successful playwright on the London stage. He was not happy in the theater, and his light subject matter and old-fashioned plots soon lost favor with critics, if not with the general audience. He turned to the novel, experimented with historical romances and picaresque stories, and then found his métier in the family novel and the three-decker saga; thus, in mid-career he set out to join the company of Anthony Trollope and John Galsworthy. To a large extent he succeeded.

R. F. DELDERFIELD

R. F. Delderfield is the first critical study of this important popular writer. It also contains the first lengthy biography of Delderfield, made possible through the kind cooperation of his widow, May Delderfield, to whom I here extend my gratitude. In the absence of any extant body of criticism on Delderfield, my pleasant task has been to read carefully the entire canon and then proceed to identify major themes, establish a critical apparatus for comparative evaluation, familiarize or refamiliarize readers with the contents of lengthy tomes, and explain the reasons, both obvious and arcane, for Delderfield's enormous popularity; for, ultimately, this study chronicles and justifies the rise to great fame of R. F. Delderfield and his brand of social-historical-familial epic in a mere fifteen-year period. It is my ultimate belief that *The Avenue Story, Diana, A Horseman Riding By, To Serve Them All My Days*, and what I call the Swann saga (*God Is an Englishman, Theirs Was the Kingdom,* and *Give Us This Day*) will find an enduring readership well into the twenty-first century, providing the British, as John Galsworthy did two generations before, with a distant mirror, and their admirers with a portrait of many a "finest hour."

In addition to thanking May Delderfield, I also extend my gratitude to several others who have helped with this book, especially Margaret Body, managing editor of Hodder and Stoughton; Dr. Wendy Bousfield; William D. West; Professor James MacKillop; Joanne Jones; DawnMaree Girndt; and last but by no means least, the Inter-Library Loan staff of Bird Library, Syracuse University.

Sanford Sternlicht

Syracuse University

Chronology

1912   Ronald Frederick Delderfield born on 12 February in New Cross, London; third son of Alice (Jones) and William James Delderfield. Family moves to Bermondsey, London.

1916   Begins elementary schooling in first of seven schools attended.

1918   Family moves to rural outer London suburban parish of Addiscombe, South Croyden.

1923   Family moves to Exmouth, Devon. Father becomes publisher of *Exmouth Chronicle*.

1926   Enrolled in West Buckland Public (private) School.

1928   General education finished at West Buckland School.

1929   Completes Fulford's Business College and assumes editorship of the *Exmouth Chronicle* from father.

1936   Marries May Evans. Settles in Exmouth.

1937   *Spark in Judea* produced in London.

1939   *Twilight Call* produced in Birmingham and *Printer's Devil* produced in London.

1940   Enlists in Royal Air Force.

1943   Receives Royal Air Force commission.

1944   Daughter Veronica adopted.

1944–1945   Military service in France and Belgium.

1945   Discharged from Royal Air Force. *Worm's Eye View* produced in London. *The Spinster of South Street* produced in London. Returns to take up permanent residence in Devon.

1946   Son, Paul, adopted. *Peace Comes to Peckham* produced in London.

1947 *All Over the Town.* Also presented in dramatic form in London.

1948 *The Queen Came By* produced in London. *Seven Men of Gascony.*

1950 *Farewell the Tranquil Mind.*

1951 *Waggonload o' Monkeys* produced in London. *Nobody Shouted Author.*

1953 *Follow the Plough* produced in London. Mother dies.

1954 *The Orchard Walls* produced in London. *Bird's Eye View.*

1956 Makes decision to disengage from the theater and pursue novelist's career. *The Adventures of Ben Gunn.* Father dies.

1957 *The Mayerling Affair* produced at Pitlochry Festival.

1958 *The Dreaming Suburb; The Avenue Goes to War.*

1959 *Napoleon in Love.*

1960 *There Was a Fair Maid Dwelling.*

1961 *Stop at a Winner.*

1962 *The Unjust Skies; The March of the Twenty-Six: The Story of Napoleon's Marshals.*

1963 *My Dearest Angel* produced at Pitlochry Festival. *The Spring Madness of Mr. Sermon.*

1964 *Too Few for Drums; Under an English Sky; The Golden Millstones: Napoleon's Brothers and Sisters.*

1966 *A Horseman Riding By.*

1967 *Cheap Day Return; The Retreat from Moscow.*

1968 *The Green Gauntlet; Imperial Sunset: The Fall of Napoleon: 1813–1814; For My Own Amusement.*

1969 *Come Home Charlie and Face Them.*

1970 *God Is an Englishman; Overture for Beginners.*

1971 *Theirs Was The Kingdom.*

1972   *To Serve Them All My Days*. Dies on 24 June in his home in Sidmouth, Devon.

1973   *Give Us This Day* published posthumously.

Chapter One
The Devon Cockney

Ronald Frederick Delderfield was born in 1912, two months before the loss of the *Titanic*. The "unsinkable," technological marvel went down on her maiden voyage, foundering on an iceberg. Fifteen hundred and thirteen people drowned and a young century received its first great shock, for science and technology, which turn-of-the-century humanity had began to substitute for religion and class structure to provide social and economic progress, had failed in a most visible and lethal way. The Edwardian afternoon was coming to an end. The disaster presaged the end of an era more dramatically than the death two years before of the beloved libertine, Edward VII, who had given his name to his time. Two years after the *Titanic*, law, reason, religion, and compassion also failed humanity and the world spent the remainder of the first half of the twentieth century in suicidal wars and economic upheaval, and then endured the terror of potential nuclear Armaggedon during the second half.

The two great pylon markers of Delderfield's life and art were the two world wars. Understandably, these wars loom large in his novels. His personal reading for pleasure centered on an earlier world conflict, the Napoleonic Wars. Among Delderfield's initial childhood memories were the sounds of falling bombs from German zeppelins in World War I. He spent six years of his life in the Royal Air Force, which, coincidentally, also came into existence in 1912.

R. F. Delderfield was the quintessentially English writer. Most of the settings of his novels and plays are English locales, reflecting the three kinds of living experiences Delderfield knew: inner-city London life, suburban London life, and West Country town life in Exmouth. He appreciated all three but came to love the last most of all as his belief grew that small-town, village, and country life were the perduring architectonics of what was and is English. London may continually metastasize wealth, power, and social problems; Birmingham, Liverpool, and Manchester may rise and fall with the economic tides, but for Delderfield the values and amenities of English life far from metropolis were those that shall not only endure but prevail.

Birth and Family

"Ronnie" Delderfield was born on 12 February 1912 in New Cross, South London, some three miles east of Bermondsey where the Delderfield family had previously lived and to which they moved back within the year. New Cross was more open then, but Delderfield's father, William James Delderfield, served as a radical member of the Bermondsey Borough Council and missed being close to the scene of the action.[1] Within a few months of Ronnie's birth the family moved back to Fort Road, S.E., into a large, roomy house with a stable yard and carriage entrance, for it had at one time been part of a district of detached houses surrounded by gardens. Now it was only a street or two from the teeming heart of cockney London.

The youngest Delderfield was the last of four sons. The first born was Ewart, named for William Ewart Gladstone, the great Liberal prime minister whose career had come to an end the year before the boy's birth in 1895. Ewart died of scarlet fever when he was only six. William was born in 1901. He was Delderfield's boyhood hero, his "Beau Geste,"[2] who served in the merchant marine in World War I and survived a torpedoing, joined the Royal Flying Corps (later the R.A.F.), emigrated to Australia after the war to become a policeman, and wound up as police commissioner of Tasmania. Delderfield always thought of big brother Bill as his "Robinson Crusoe, Don Quixote, Long John Silver, Huckleberry Finn, Ghengis Khan, Marco Polo, Richard the Lion-heart, and Peter the Whaler. . . ."(*OFB*, 44).

Eric, who remained a friend, companion, and advisor to his younger brother, came eight years after Bill.

The elder Delderfield, a lifelong radical, hero-worshiped Abraham Lincoln, and when his fourth son was born on the Great Emancipator's birthday, he took it as a sign and "nearly went mad with joy."[3] The child was to be named Abraham Lincoln Delderfield. Mrs. Delderfield, a politically as well as religiously conservative Welsh woman, objected strenuously. The couple had agreed to alternate the right to choose the names of their offspring. It was her turn, sign or no sign. Father Delderfield recognized the fatuity of dissent. The child was christened Ronald Frederick and nicknamed Ronnie. In adult life friends and associates called him Ron.

Delderfield's father was the first and perhaps the greatest influence on his life. The author considered his father "the most colorful, complex and contradictory character I have ever met. . . . He baffled, bewildered and exasperated every human being who crossed his path . . . not because he enjoyed . . . throwing his personality at strangers as though it was a large custard pie, but because . . . he had a rooted conviction that everybody needed him to solve their personal problems and shape their judgements."[4]

William James Delderfield was born in Bermondsey in 1873, the eldest son of an intemperate tanner who fathered a Victorian brood of six daughters and two sons in a small house. He was at work at thirteen, laboring for a Tower Bridge tea importer and using both cunning and fists to survive in the slums of London. At sixteen he succeeded his father as head of household, got work in the leather trade as a flesher, and then entered the meat trade in London's famous Smithfield Market where he progressed from clerk to sales manager. At twenty-one he took the pledge to battle "Daemon Rum," joined the local Congregational chapel, and entered politics as a radical Liberal, being elected to the Bermondsey Borough Council the same year. He was a fiery speaker, a "Thames-side Lloyd George," an anti−Boer War spokesperson, an ardent churchgoer forever dragging his reluctant sons to Sunday school and Baptist chapel, and an implacable enemy of Tories, Freemasons, landlords, nobles, bishops, and brewers. He lived eighty-three cantankerous years, dying in 1956.

From childhood on Delderfield's reaction to and relationship with his strong father was ambivalent. He rejected his father's political extremism, his religious intolerance, his militancy, and his extrovertism; but he embraced his concern for Britain's future, his dedication to truth, his integrity, his pride in being English, and his courage. For in 1923 the elder Delderfield threw up his Smithfield career and without any journalistic experience bought a small-town weekly newspaper in a region of England generally opposed to his political views. He not only succeeded in his venture, but his action was eventually responsible for the creation of the writer R. F. Delderfield.

Delderfield's mother, Alice Jones Delderfield, was the only daughter of a Welsh family living in London. Her parents had come from Devil's Bridge, Aberystwyth, and had moved to the capital in the 1850s seeking economic advantages. Alice's father had also worked in the London tea trade. Alice was well bred and well read, being passionately devoted to Shakespeare and Dickens. She was a reserved, unemotional woman whose personality balanced the mercurial, choloric nature of her husband. Requiring little in the way of social life, and disliking housework, she proved to be an excellent business-woman when the family went into publishing (*BEV*, 8–9).

Move to the Suburbs

In 1915 and 1916 London was under air attack from German zeppelins. Among Delderfield's earliest memories was that of a policeman blowing his whistle and shouting "Take Cover!" and people screaming as they ran for shelter. One raid, which dropped an aerial torpedo nearby, wiping out a row of houses, demolished Alice's nerves, and William James reluctantly decided to leave his beloved cockney London after some forty-five years and move his family to a neat new terraced row house, 22 Ashburton Avenue in Addiscombe, a suburb of Croyden, some dozen miles from the center of London, then a part of the great green outer suburban ring of the metropolis (*BEV*, 14–15).

South Croyden was a wonderland to the six-year-old liberated from the inner city. For the first time the young Delderfield could see seasonal changes, giant oaks, vast green meadows, birds flying overhead, and fat cattle grazing. His imagination stirred. Simultaneously, however, as he came to love the English countryside, Delderfield came to know the English class system, for unlike cockney London, the suburb of Croyden was the kingdom of the "arrived," those immigrants to the middle class who, by dint of an extra pound or two per week, guarded their new status like Rhine gold, seldom talked to their neighbors on their own street, and never spoke to those who lived in what they considered "lesser addresses." They sent their young children to private "colleges" to avoid the council schools where their offspring might have to consort with working-class children, even though the public institutions were often superior to the private ones.

Alice Delderfield sent Eric to a private grammar school but Ronnie was sent to the local council school because he was too young for grammar school and because it appears that the family was somewhat financially strained by the move to Croyden. Delderfield found life in his new school oppressive. The cane was administered unsparingly. The building was something of a Victorian barracks. The children were frequently poorly fed and dressed. However, the curriculum was more demanding than what Delderfield had faced in his first school in Bermondsey and the boy knuckled down to hard study. At this time he was diagnosed as being nearsighted and was fitted for glasses. Delderfield wore eyeglasses for the remainder of his life, first rolled-gold framed, then tortoiseshell as a teenager, and finally horn-rimmed as an adult. They gave him something of an owlish countenance.

Mrs. Delderfield soon began to feel social embarrassment in regard to Ronnie's schooling. They had made the move to the suburbs in part for the benefit of their children and it seemed contradictory to have their youngest son remain in an educational environment no different from the one he had left in Central London. Mr. Delderfield accompanied Ronnie to Selhurst Grammar School, four miles away on the far side of Croyden, where Eric was studying. There they met the gowned headmaster, who gave the boy an oral exam and found him intelligent and learned enough for admission. The school for five hundred sons of the suburbs was well-run and had a large and competent staff. Discipline was more moderate. It was of the "right class." There were piano lessons at home for further "gentifying." Only, unfortunately for the Delderfields, Ronnie's cockney accent had taken. His inner-London origins remained apparent all his life.

It was shortly after his admission to Selhurst Grammar, and per-haps not unrelated to that event—for the masters were academically demanding and Ronnie had to live down his brother's reputation as a cut, time-waster, and traditional bad boy—that he entered a period of deep depression which he described as a "sort of rarified persecution-complex that had as its driving force a compelling masochism, a merciless insistance on doing, saying, and confessing things that were certain to cause me reproaches and condemnation" (*BEV*, 43). For many months he lived in dread of being buried alive unless he performed certain self-appointed tasks that would, like a talisman, ward off his fate. The depression passed just before the family moved again.

During this formative suburban period in Delderfield's life he became passionately and irrevocably addicted to movies. The films took all his spending money and much of his time. His parents tried various prohibitions to curb Ronnie's insatiable appetite for silent films and then the talkies, but they finally gave up in defeat. Later Delderfield's wife shared the addiction. In war and peace, in sickness and health, under stress or on holiday, a visit to the cinema was sure to help matters.

The final influence of the Croyden period on Delderfield was the Baptist chapel. Although Delderfield claimed no spiritual benefit from the forced attendance at his father's church, and eventually moved to the Congregationalists and ultimately to his mother's Anglican church, it was through an event at chapel that the ten-year-old came to know that he "would have to spin English words on a thread and that no other occupation made would make the least appeal to me" (*FMOA*, 88). He had heard a professional elocutionist, one John Torceni, give a reading in a chapel concert. The material from Dickens, Kingsley, Tennyson, Conrad, and Goldsmith enthralled the youth. Drunk on language, his head always reeling with motion picture images, the boy was on his way to becoming a writer. Torceni had decided how Delderfield would spend his days (*FMOA*, 88).

Devon

In 1923 the fifty-year-old senior Delderfield decided that he wanted to get away from the London fog and from the early rising required in the meat trade. Today one might say he had a mid-life crisis. Along with a neighbor he bought a business in Devon: a printing works, a stationery store, and a weekly newspaper, The *Exmouth Chronicle*, all located in a single building, called Berlin House, situated on the main street of Exmouth. He knew nothing of the printing or paper business and little about newspapers except that he read several daily. However, he never doubted but that he would be a competent editor. The *Chronicle* eventually provided the vehicle for R. F. Delderfield's writing apprenticeship.

Alice Delderfield was delighted at the thought of helping with the business and having a maid to do all the chores she disliked. Eric and Ronnie were brought to Exmouth on Christmas Eve 1923. The family moved into an apartment on the top floor of the works.

Exmouth provided a romantic background for the impressionable eleven-year-old. It was a small coastal town of some ten thousand souls with a single dock and two or three streets of shops. Many of the residents were retired civil servants and soldiers who had served the Empire in the four corners of the British world. There were boat yards and timber yards and sail-driven coasters with salty skippers and crews. Delderfield thought himself the most fortunate boy in the world (*BEV*, 58).

Eric was delighted to learn that he would not have to return to school, but would be apprenticed to the printing trade. Ronnie was enrolled in the local "secondary school" appropriate for his age. To his delight it was coeducational. Girls, however, got him into the first real trouble of his life. It was called "The Brickworks Scandal." Delderfield and some friends were caught kissing girls in an abandoned brickyard. It was a trivial, really absurd, incident, but the school authorities threatened expulsion and the senior Delderfield, always somewhat of a puritan, decided that coeducation was morally suspect and Delderfield was shunted off to a notable public school, the West Buckland School, in North Devon.

Delderfield's educational experiences at West Buckland were the best he had in the seven schools he attended. Boarding school took him away from his sometimes domineering but otherwise busy and indifferent father whose only advice to his departing son was to avoid associating with "dirty-minded boys" (*BEV*, 79).

At West Buckland Delderfield made lifelong "old boy" friends, learned to play cricket badly, to run cross country, to dress as a young gentleman, and to attend Church of England services. The latter two activities delighted his mother and appalled his father. That militant pacifist gentleman also objected to his son's joining the officers' training corps. West Buckland introduced Delderfield to the stage. As his voice had not changed, he was given the part of Inez, the aged nurse, in Gilbert and Sullivan's *The Gondoliers*. Alas, he fell down a flight of stairs before his entrance, came on dazed, and was struck by the descending final curtain to the great delight of the audience (*BEV*, 102).

Most important of all, there were good and dedicated masters at West Buckland who encouraged Delderfield's writing. After all, he was going to inherit a newspaper someday, and journalism, if not belletristic writing, it seemed would be his lifelong career. In fact, his writing had been noted and encouraged earlier. At the previous school, in Exmouth, the English master had encouraged Delderfield by publishing some of his doggerel verses in the school magazine. One poem was about a dog and another about a dentist. There was also a short story about the French Revolution indicating the very beginning of the author's lifelong interest in the history of the Revolution and the Napoleonic period. The creative work received much praise and the boy began to think about writing as a shortcut to fame and fortune (*BEV*, 65). He had learned that printing would be his brother's part in the family business and editing and journalism his. Perhaps newspaper work could be a springboard for higher literary goals.

Further encouraged to write at West Buckland, Delderfield turned out a dramatic thriller, "Murder in the Pulpit," which was produced at the school. Delderfield was rewarded with a half hour off from homework.

Years later Delderfield looked back on his days at West Buckland as among the happiest of his life. There he indulged his love for reading, for literature was a major part of the curriculum and it was well taught. Among the great books Delderfield enjoyed reading and studying were *The Mill on the Floss, The Vicar of Wakefield*, and *The Count of Monte Cristo*. Delderfield also read most of Dickens during this period of his life. In 1963 Delderfield compiled and introduced *Tales Out of School: An Anthology of West Buckland Reminiscences 1885– 1963* in which he wrote movingly of his teachers and friends, reflecting: "Did the sun shine more often then or is this youthful fantasy? . . . I loved the sense of belonging and the invigorating moorland air, the antics in and out of class and the excitements on the sports field, the pride of wearing an ill-fitting military uniform on Corps day and the friendliness of the local people. . . ."[5] Delderfield even wrote an alternate school song, ending: "Homing on Buckland, timeless and ageless, Evermore changing, ever the same" (*TOS*, 78).

Exmouth Editor

As his youngest and most literary son approached his seventeenth birthday, the elder Delderfield decided that the youth had had enough general education and that it was time for Ronnie to prepare for work. He took his son out of West Buckland and enrolled him in Fulford's Business College in nearby Exeter where Delderfield studied bookkeeping, shorthand, and typing (*BEV*, 116; *FMOA*, 160). Simultaneously, on the weekends he worked for the *Chronicle* (circulation 2,000–3,000) as a folder in the printing plant and as a bill collector. At the latter task he failed miserably and soon was delivering papers instead.

As soon as the commercial college course, which Delderfield rather enjoyed only because it was coed and he was one of three males in a roomful of flappers, was completed, he joined the *Chronicle* full-time as reporter and subeditor. His beats included all the local weddings and funerals, making sure to get all facts right and names spelled correctly. He acted as order clerk for the printing department showing wedding announcements. As the *Chronicle*'s court reporter he attended petty sessions at the little courthouse behind the Exmouth police station. Evangelist revivals and meetings of the local council government had to be reported. Best of all, however, was the opportunity to interview celebrities vacationing at nearby coastal resorts. Delderfield's prize catch was an interview with the elusive George Bernard Shaw.

Before he was eighteen Delderfield found himself sole editor of the *Exmouth Chronicle*. His father had decided that he had worked long and hard enough and at fifty-six he turned the business operation over to Ron and Eric, spending much of the rest of his life traveling around the world with his wife on money his sons earned for him. When his father casually told him of his new responsibility, Delderfield thought, "It was rather like a skylarking longshoreman vacating the bridge of an Atlantic liner and handing over to the cabin boy" (*FMOA*, 42). However, Delderfield quickly became an excellent provincial journalist and editor. He revamped the format of the *Chronicle* and sharpened editorial comment.

Looking back in 1954 to the events of 1929 Delderfield noted that from the beginning he was less than happy with being anchored seemingly permanently at so early an age: "The more I thought

about my anchorage the less I liked it. . . . I saw myself, old, grey
and obese, standing in the same spot as that I now occupied, and
going through an identical set of movements over the supplements of
the 1972 issues" (*BEV*, 132). Ironically, the year of ultimate boredom Delderfield selected, his sixtieth, would be the year of his
death. But he died a renown writer, not a small-town editor.

Apprentice Playwright

For some time Delderfield considered trying for a career as a Fleet
Street reporter in London, but the depression years did not encourage
young people to throw up secure livelihoods on the mere chance of
more satisfying careers. Having read and occasionally seen plays, and
believing that successful playwrights such as Robert Cedric Sherriff,
author of the great war play *Journey's End*, had rocketed to fame on
the strength of a single play and led lives of leisure, travel, and
freedom, Delderfield naively decided that he would write "a successful play." It turned out to be a piece about the Napoleonic period
unfortunately titled "One More Bed." The play was entered in a
contest and Delderfield received enough encouragement to continue
writing dramas. However, nine years passed before a Delderfield play
was given a London production in an outlying theater in July 1939.
By that time he had written fifteen three-act plays, many one-acters,
five novels, and an autobiography. Delderfield's apprenticeship as
both playwright and novelist was a long, hard, and somewhat un-
lucky one.

During the early newspaper years Delderfield read everything he
could get his hands on about Napoleon and the Napoleonic period.
He collected Napoleonic books and he wrote a series of tales, never
published, called "The Adventures of Coronet Cavendish," an imita-
tion of Arthur Conan Doyle's *Adventures of Gerard* (*BEV*, 142–43).

Desperate to achieve something in print Delderfield also tried
songwriting and commercial jingles. For one hit, a rhyme for
Wright's Coal Tar Soap, he earned a pound:

> On Friday Night it's Ma's delight
> To bathe us all at leisure,
> For Wright's Coal Tar, says dear old Ma,
> Makes bathing us a pleasure.

(*BEV*, 144)

It was his first pay for writing outside of journalism. An advertising agent sent him a box of chocolates for another piece. The pound postal order and the candy represented his total "creative" earnings for many years despite the tens of thousands of words he wrote.

However, play writing was Delderfield's chief literary activity in the period prior to 1939. He wrote play after play, long and short, and sent them to contests, theater managers, and agents. He sometimes received encouragement but never achieved either production or publication until 1937, and he received very little recognition until after World War II. Nevertheless the dream lingered on.

Courtship and Marriage

In the summer of 1930 Delderfield and his brother Eric decided to take a first vacation together since childhood, warily leaving father temporarily in charge of the business. The lads went to North Wales with a few pounds to spend and Delderfield's ukulele to serenade any girls they might meet. They stayed in a youth hostel and met two young ladies about their own age. One of them, a slim, high cheek-boned beauty with pageboy, bobbed chestnut hair, caught Delderfield's fancy with the demure look he apparently preferred for his heroines in real life as well as fiction. Her name was May Evans and she was a laboratory assistant from the Manchester suburb of Rusholme. They spent a pleasant week together, had a single exchange of letters upon returning home, and then ceased to correspond for more than a year.

The following summer Delderfield received a letter from May requesting the name, price, and publisher of the new novel he had brought out, because her co-workers had expressed curiosity about a living author. She said she did not know what he wrote and had assumed he was a novelist. Perhaps she wished for an excuse to renew the acquaintance? Delderfield immediately wrote back that there had been some slight delay in his achieving publication, and a four-year romance, mostly by letter—some 1,400 in fact—ensued. They met occasionally in London or in a small town halfway between Exmouth and Manchester whenever there was a cheap rail fare available and their budgets allowed. Engagement came on Christmas night, 1934.

A year and a half later, in March 1936, despite driving his car off the road and sustaining a mashed nose two nights before the wedding, Ronald married May in Manchester in a registry office; they honeymooned in London, going to the theater every night. They then returned to Exmouth where Delderfield resumed his editorship and May set up housekeeping in a rented three-bedroom house. Soon afterwards they moved to a four-bedroom house, inexplicably called "Oak Park," where they could let out a room or two to summer visitors. They resided in Exmouth until Delderfield's war service, at which time May followed her husband to several bases when he was still stationed in England. When Delderfield was sent overseas she returned to Exmouth.

The couple lived their entire married life on the Devon Coast either in Exmouth, Pebblecombe Regis, Budleigh Salterton, or Sidmouth. Their marriage was a happy and peaceful one, marred only by May's three stillbirths, the last coming while Delderfield was on active duty in the winter of 1942–43. Finally, they decided to adopt. Veronica came in 1944, shortly after the last stillbirth, and Paul was adopted in 1946 just after Delderfield's first commercial success in the theater, *Worm's Eye View*. May became an expert on antiques and early on helped supplement the family income with deft purchases and sales.

After settling down in "Oak Park" Delderfield wrote a play about his experiences as a small-town editor, first calling it "Fleet Street in Lilliput" and later "Printer's Devil." In the meantime, however, an earlier play, *Spark in Judea*, unbeknown to Delderfield, had been passed on to a society named "New Plays" and the director decided to give it an afternoon's production on an autumn Sunday in 1937. Delighted, Delderfield and May came up to see a play of his performed for the first time. They were ecstatic and he was hooked on the theater. "Printer's Devil" received good notices in a subsequent experimental theater production in London in 1939. Delderfield believed that at long last he was on his way to a career in the theater. Fringe of London successes boded well for a West End opportunity. Alas for his plans, and the hopes and dreams of millions, World War II intervened.

Royal Air Force

In April 1940 Delderfield, a married, unathletically built, tall, balding intellectual, joined the long lines of patriotic Britons joining the services. He chose the Royal Air Force and was trained for clerical duties. As a clerk he was shunted from one backwater base to another, some eighteen of them in all, drowning for three years in the boredom of supply and personnel work. He tried for a commission but was initially turned down because his education was considered inadequate for an officer. Flying, of course, was out of the question with his weak eyes. His wartime ennui provided material for the hit play *Worm's Eye View* (1944)[6] and the novel *Stop at a Winner* (1961). Finding the boredom unbearable he volunteered for the bomb disposal squad but to no avail. The R.A.F. held on to him. One activity helped; he wrote and directed camp shows. On one occasion he was sent over to the famous Birmingham Repertory Theatre to borrow scenery, obtaining several truckloads full. A few nights later the theater was destroyed in an air raid. Delderfield had inadvertently saved much of its stock (*BEV*, 223).

In the R.A.F. Delderfield continued to write plays and to hope for productions. Max Reinhardt, the great German director in exile in New York, promised a production of *Spark in Judea* but died before the production got under way. Delderfield struggled on, was hospitalized for shingles, and promoted to corporal. He continued to try for a commission and more meaningful service. Finally, in November 1943, he was sent to an officers' cadet school for a commissioning course, but not before he had hit upon the idea for a play based on the conflict between uniformed personnel and contemptuous civilians. He quickly wrote down the synopsis for *Worm's Eye View*, the story of five airmen in a civilian billet in 1942–43. He did not realize it at the time, but his experience as an enlisted man provided him material much later as a writer.

In February 1944, after a brief tour as an assistant camp adjutant, Flight Lieutenant Delderfield was posted to the Air Ministry in London to work as a public relations officer. At last he had an assignment somewhat related to his skills as a journalist and writer. Stationed at Whitehall, in the heart of London, he found himself in the company of other writers, some of whom became lifelong friends, including the novelist H. E. Bates, the biographer Dudley Barker, the poet John Pudney, and the lexicographer Eric Partridge. At first he wrote press releases pseudonymously and finished *Worm's Eye View*, which he mailed to the producer Basil Thomas. Happy to leave behind the V1 bombs blitzing London in the summer of 1944, Delderfield was flown to the Continent, his first trip away from Britain, to cover the fall of the city of Le Harve to the advancing Allies. He was accompanied by a famous press photographer and raconteur, Stanley Devon, about whom he wrote a monograph, *These Clicks Made History: The Story of Stanley ("Glorious") Devon, Fleet Street Photographer* (1946). Returning home, he was immediately flown back to the Continent in charge of a reconnaisance team ordered to report on the effects of Allied bombing on fifty-six targets in France and Belgium. It was the greatest adventure of Delderfield's life and more background for *Stop at a Winner*. His six-man team lived off the countryside denuded by retreating Germans and advancing Allies and got caught up in the backwash of the Battle of the Bulge. In his kit Delderfield packed five favorite books for traveling companions: Robert Louis Stevenson's *Treasure Island*, to which he was addicted from childhood (*FMOA*, 269); Thomas Carlyle's *French Revolution*, whose prose he considered masterful; Mark Twain's *Huckleberry Finn*, to save his sense of humor; Baron de Marbot's *Memoirs*, which continually freshened his love for the Napoleonic; and Helen Ashton's *Doctor Serecold*, a book that satisfied his need for narrative. Often he was exhausted and without food, but the books were never bartered or abandoned.

Meanwhile, unbeknown to Delderfield, Basil Thomas had produced *Bird's Eye View* in October 1944 at the Wolverhamton Grand Theatre. When Delderfield finally got his outfit to Paris in January 1945 a batch of fifty letters were waiting for him acclaiming the production he knew nothing about (*BEV*, 256).

Back home at the Air Ministry Flight Lieutenant Delderfield found himself an authority on bombing (*OFB*, 197) but was more interested in learning the fate of his play. It had had a good week's run in repertory and there was the hope of a London production. In April 1945, it began a six-town tryout tour. Reception was mixed. Meanwhile Delderfield's play about Florence Nightingale, *The Spinster of South Street* (1945), was also touring provincial theaters but it faded with poor reviews. A London West End production of *Worm's Eye View* began to seem like a dream, despite the enthusiasm of actors and directors.

Civvy Street

In November 1945, almost three months after the Japanese surrendered to end World War II, Flight Lieutenant Delderfield was mustered out of the service at Wembley Stadium along with his friend H. E. Bates. There was nothing for him to do but to return to

Exmouth, May, two-year-old Veronica, and the *Chronicle*. Soon he was back in the old routine: weddings, funerals, council meetings, and sales. But *Worm's Eye View* refused to die. A producer gambled on a four-week London run starting 4 December 1945. Reviews were ecstatic. The play closed in June 1951 after a run of five years, seven months. It broke the London straight play record and the all-time British performance record.

Delderfield was now Britain's "hottest" playwright. The brothers sold the *Chronicle* in February 1947. Delderfield could not be a journalist and a full-time playwright simultaneously, and enough royalty money was coming in to allow the writer and his family, now four with the addition of Paul, to live quite comfortably in a large house on the Devon coast with domestic help. He worked in his study at a furious pace, one which he kept up for the rest of his life, writing an incredible 4,000 words every day, 365 days a year, working mornings and evenings with mid-day off for exercise. His top one-day production was 5,200 words.

Plays seemed to tumble from his typewriter, some produced, others not. None ever attained the popularity or critical success of *Worm's Eye View*. Among those achieving London productions were *Peace Comes to Peckham* (1946), *All Over the Town* (1947), *The Queen Came By* (1948), and *Waggonload o' Monkeys* (1951). Two dramas were produced at the Pitlochry Festival after London producers and managers stopped doing his plays: *The Mayerling Affair* (1957) and *My Dearest Angel* (1963). He had not realized it at the time, but the success of *Bird's Eye View* was not only the beginning of his career as a professional playwright, it was the high water mark. Fortunately, Delderfield also decided in the immediate postwar period to try his hand at the novel as well as drama, writing *All Over Town* (1947), based on his experiences as a small-town journalist; *Seven Men of Gascony* (1949), a story of the French army in the Napoleonic Wars; and *Farewell, the Tranquil Mind* (1950), a tale of an Englishman trapped in Revolutionary France. In the latter two works Delderfield demonstrated his ability both to write romantic historical novels and to employ his lifelong study of Napoleonic France.

The Delderfields' life-style changed fairly quickly. They tried some farming at Pebblecombe Regis, and Delderfield wrote amusingly about their failure in *Nobody Shouted Author* (1951). Upon the advice of a physician friend who loved horses, Delderfield took up riding and then fox hunting. He became proficient at riding and grew to love the hunt. His life became the antithesis of his father's. The estate living, the fox hunting, the antique collecting seemed to indicate that Delderfield was unconsciously rejecting the radicalism of his father and distancing himself from the working-class and lower-middle- class values and environs of his parents, uncles, and aunts—particularly his father's family. Delderfield was not really comfortable as an enlisted man in the R.A.F. although his experiences in the ranks provided him with much of his material for his early plays and novels: "No matter how fervently it may be denied the English are still a class-ridden society. With the best will in the world there remains a gulf between the man born into a family that is comfortable off and the man whose father brought home a weekly wage and parted with most of it for the housekeeping. I did not believe this when I first met men who had never wanted for money but I believe it now."[7] His establishment writer friends during his Air Ministry service urged him "to exploit the literary and dramatic advantage I had in nearly four years as an aircraftman second class, an aircraftman first class, a leading aircraftman and a corporal" (*FMOA*, 1968, 215).

One conjectures that the long pursuit of a military commission, the squire's life in a succession of Devon country houses, the fox hunting, the high church Anglican affiliation, the personal reserve, and the exalting of the countryside in his novels were manifestations of Delderfield's rejection of the radical popularism of his ideologic father, the senior Delderfield's Baptist convictions, and the control the dogmatic parent exercised over his youngest son. Delderfield could not help but feel that his father's political radicalism and familial authoritarianism were contradictory if not hypocritical.

Thus, partly in reaction to his father's politics and partly because of his own experiences as a journalist and an airman, Delderfield developed and incorporated into his writing a centrist view of an improved if not ideal British society. Although he made no direct political statements, Delderfield's politics clearly were conservatively Liberal, eschewing the Conservative–Labor polarization that developed after World War II. He hoped for slow, orderly change and continued measured improvement in the quality of British life with change evolving peacefully and not impinging on the traditions of his nation. To him the British class structure was not an evil but a strength, a part of what architectonically held together the body politic, with each class, something of a separate tribe, respecting the

other classes but maintaining proudly its own customs and traditions. The ideal society for Britain was not an egalitarian one but an
harmonious one.

The death of Delderfield's parents, his mother in 1952 and his
father in 1956, along with the lack of commercial success for his
most recent plays, caused Delderfield to reconsider his life's work.
His father at fifty had tergiversated, giving up a secure, salaried
position in meat for the more romantic life of a newspaper publisher,
and six years later he gave up that life for that of a world traveler and
observer of life. Delderfield was never really happy in the theater. He
did not get along all that well with producers and actors and he
wrote about them satirically.[8] Later he complained that "he changed
to fiction . . . because actors were forever changing his lines
and . . . fiction editors asked permission merely to change punctua-
tion."[9] He grew cynical of reviewers and press agents who in quoting
from notices could "so manipulate the words and the full-stops that a
'stinker' can be disguised as a rave" (*NSA*, 144).

The Delderfields did not enjoy spending much time in London and
they seldom took trips to the Continent and the United States, the
latter only for business. They had become country people, and if
horseback riding was Delderfield's most pleasureable recreation,
May's was driving about the country to house sales and purchasing
antiques. A play became "a prolonged charade. If one sought enlight-
enment or mental enlargement then one went to a book and turned
the pages slowly, pondering the wisdom therein" (*FMOA*, 367). By
continuing to reside in Devon instead of London, they had chosen to
live among the people they knew and liked and could trust. The
terrain was familiar, rich in atmosphere, and inhabited by a plethora
of possible story characters. Thus in 1956, at the age of forty-four,
ten years after he had embarked on a full-time career as a playwright,
Delderfield changed course, making the novel the center of his writing.

Novelist

The commitment to the novel began with *The Avenue Story*, which
records the life of a suburban community from 1919 through 1947.
It was published in two parts: *The Dreaming Suburb* (1958) and *The
Avenue Goes to War* (1958). Meticulously, Delderfield prepared by
beginning with a detailed map, actually numbering the houses on an

avenue and carefully plotting out the lives of the inhabitants of each
domicile, allowing, Pirandello-like, for his characters to share with
their author the unraveling of their fates (*FMOA*, 286). As to philosophy and profound messages, Delderfield was fond of quoting his
movie hero Humphrey Bogart: "If a writer has a message he should
ring up Western Union" (*FMOA*, 285). From the beginning of the
period of his dedication to the novel, the author felt that "The
primary objective of a writer of fiction should be to entertain and
divert. Anything else that emerges from his work is a bonus"
(*FMOA*, 285). Of course, there are many bonuses for the reader in
Delderfield's work, but they are coterminous with and subsidiary to
the craft of storytelling. Delderfield's main goal was to "project the
English way of life in the tradition of Hardy and Galsworthy." [10]

There Was a Fair Maid Dwelling (1960) followed *The Avenue Story*.
It was published in America the same year as *Diana* and was a
Literary Guild selection. The sequel, *The Unjust Skies* (1962), did not
receive American publication until 1972. The two books were later
published together as *Diana* in Britain and produced as a television
series. With it Delderfield began to develop an American audience.
Still experimenting with subject and approach, Delderfield wrote
three very different novels in rapid succession: *Stop at a Winner*
(1961), the comic adventure of two R.A.F. buddies based on his own
experiences in the service; *The Spring Madness of Mr. Sermon* (1963), J.
B. Priestley-like comedy about a fifty-year-old man (Delderfield's age
at the time) who is having a mid-life crisis; and *Too Few for Drums*
(1964), the romantic tale of a young English army officer trapped
behind French lines in the Penninsular War. None of these books
made a great impact. The next one did.

A Horseman Riding By (1966) and its sequel, *The Green Gauntlet*
(1968), mark the triumph of Delderfield the novelist. Over fifteen
hundred pages of saga proved that Delderfield could write the sweep-
ing, generations-enfolding family epic that the English audience so
admired in John Galsworthy's chronicles of the Forsyte family and
Arnold Bennett's treatment of the Clayhangers. Additionally,
Delderfield's central positing of the Devonshire landscape evoked
comparison with Thomas Hardy's treatment of Dorset. The saga also
received a British television series production.

Once more, as with *The Avenue*, Delderfield began with a map.
This time it was an entire landscape complete with farms, woods,
roads, rivers, and coves. He randomly plucked a hundred names from

the telephone book for his characters and created a thirty-eight-year history for the Sorrell Valley. Oddly, Delderfield had trouble placing *A Horseman Riding By* with an American publisher despite its success in Britain and despite the earlier success of *Diana* with the American audience. Fourteen American publishers rejected the book as too long. Fortunately, Simon & Schuster's editor Robert Gottlieb picked up a copy of it in a Piccadilly bookstore, read it, and decided to publish it in America.[11] Two more single volume novels followed: *Cheap Day Return* (1967), a love story about a middle-aged man reminiscing; and an amusing, crime story, *Come Home Charlie and Face Them* (1969). But Delderfield was warming up for his longest epic: the Swann saga.

Napoleon

From school days onward, Delderfield was entranced by Napoleon and his period. He spent much of his life researching the great French emperor and in the course of time Delderfield developed an historian's knowledge of his hero, and he used this knowledge both to write certain of his novels and parts of novels and to produce reputable popular histories. *Napoleon in Love* (1959) details the emperor's quest for romantic fulfillment. *The March of the Twenty-six: The Story of Napoleon's Marshals* (1962), profiles the emperor's key military commanders. *The Golden Millstones: Napoleon's Brothers and Sisters* (1964) tells the story of the variously endowed four brothers and three sisters of Napoleon, their influence on the ruler, the problems they caused him, and their fates. *The Retreat from Moscow* (1967) is the story of the 179 days between 24 June 1812, when the Grand Army headed east, and 19 December, when the last man of the wretched rear guard staggered out of Russia. Finally, *Imperial Sunset: The Fall of Napoleon, 1813-1814* (1968) treats the history of the sixteen months following Napoleon's retreat from Moscow.

Delderfield's admiration for the French conqueror seems contrary to his hatred for Hitler, considering that both men were England's bitter foe and both attempted total conquest and absorption of Europe. Yet Delderfield felt that if Napoleon had won there would have been a common market in Europe by 1820. His British patriotism clashed with his sense of being a European. As a European the author deplored the lack of unity that led to the terrible wars of the twentieth century. As a Briton he could not accept foreign hegemony, but Delderfield was able to justify his regard for Napoleon by noting that the emperor was himself an admirer of the English, who wanted to reside in England and become an English gentleman after his defeat. [12]

Last Work

R. F. Delderfield was a heavy smoker who continued the habit despite the urging of his wife and physician to quit. Perhaps sensing that his life was not to be a very long one, Delderfield wrote a hurricane of words in his last three years. He planned and almost completed what is his longest work, the Swann trilogy, which would have been a pentalogy had he lived longer. [13] As it is, the Swann saga—*God Is an Englishman* (1970), *Theirs Was the Kingdom* (1971), and the posthumously published *Give Us This Day* (1973)— comprises some 2,300 pages. Delderfield sandwiched in his fine tribute to the English public school and public schoolmaster, *To Serve Them All My Days* (1972), a mere 624 pages. This work is Delderfield's finest single volume story. It was also turned into a particularly successful television series.

Delderfield's last home was a rebuilt coach house called the Gazebo. It dates originally from the time of Trafalgar, and it is in Sidmouth on the Devon coast. From its windows Delderfield could see where the first galleys of the Spanish Armada were sunk by that Devon marauder, Francis Drake, and where the invasion fleet of Napoleon would have appeared and perhaps that of Hitler too. Behind the house stretches the moors where a man and his dog could walk for hours. In that English setting R. F. Delderfield died of lung cancer on 24 June 1972.

Chapter Two
First Stage

R. F. Delderfield's career as a professional creative writer overlapped his career as a journalist. It began with a long apprenticeship in writing plays, which to a very large extent Delderfield taught himself. For six years the determined author turned out play after play and sent them to agents and contest judges. Although there were encouragements, it was not until 1937 that one of his plays, *Spark in Judea*, had a fringe theater production, and it took another eight years to achieve a commercial hit, *Worm's Eye View* (1944), during its second time around in 1945. Although *Worm's Eye View* was a phenomenal success, no other play of Delderfield's was nearly as well received, and eventually the West End stopped producing his plays, although Delderfield lost interest in it before it lost interest in him.

In all R. F. Delderfield wrote thirteen full-length plays and fifteen one-acters, the latter designed for production by amateur theatrical societies. As a reporter Delderfield had seen many local productions, and he was fond of the efforts of such groups although he realized their limitations (*NSA*, 148–53). In writing one-act plays Delderfield made sure that there were many, and significant, parts for women, knowing that the typical drama is written by a man with men in mind as protagonists, but community theater groups usually have many more actresses than actors available.

Delderfield's major contribution to the drama is in his introduction of working-class characters as protagonists in English comedy, replacing the middle-class and upper-class heroes and heroines of Noël Coward, James M. Barrie, Somerset Maugham, and Frederick Lonsdale, the major British comedy writers of the pre—World War II period. This contribution, a product of the egalitarianism experienced by the author and his generation during the war years, exerted a far-reaching influence well into the 1950s and beyond. Playwrights like John Osborne and Arnold Wesker of the rebellious movement in British letters called "the Angry Young Men" found the theater environment more hospitable than it would have been, thanks to the pioneer work of Delderfield. They took the working-class setting, themes, and structure of Delderfield and his imitators and turned them into a theater of politics, transforming the disillusionment and dissatisfaction of Delderfield's generation of war veterans into the frustration of their own generation of outsiders.

The working-class and underclass settings of Harold Pinter's black comedies such as *The Birthday Party* (1958) and *The Caretaker* (1960) are on a direct continuum from the immediate postwar plays of Delderfield, which in their restrained bitterness, their self-criticism, and their simple, unaffected style and dialogue challenged the establishment in the artistic, social, and political arenas.

Prewar Plays

Spark in Judea (1937) was the first Delderfield play to be performed, receiving a one-night semiprofessional production in London by a society called New Plays (*BEV*, 194—96). It is a melodramatic version of Pontius Pilate's dilemma concerning the trial of Jesus. Pilate, a just and decent Roman official, in a difficult assignment and bothered by an unhappy socialite wife, has met the Nazarene before, when he was in despair and contemplating suicide. Jesus dissuaded him with talk of the need to continue the search for the meaning of life. Now Pilate does not want to condemn Jesus but is forced to by the High Priest of Jerusalem, who fears the disruptive power of Jesus.

Pilate is stunned that the people chose to have Barabbas pardoned and Jesus executed. He conveys his feelings of disbelief and guilt to Procula, his wife, who commiserates with him:

> Procula: You did your best to save the man before.
>
> Pilate: A coward's best. At first his life or death was a matter of common justice, but as their determination to sacrifice him hardened, so my understanding of him and his plan clarified, until I saw beyond doubt that the woman of Magdala was right—this carpenter is no conjuring Messiah, neither is he what they make him, a god. He is more. He is you, he is me, he is the whole of enslaved humanity.[1]

It is at this point in the play that the hitherto obvious plot turns interesting and the work departs from the province of Sunday school drama, for Pilate enters into a conspiracy with the followers of Jesus to have him taken down from the Cross before he is dead. The plan only partially succeeds, for Jesus dies in the arms of his friends, and Pilate is crushed by the loss of the man who could have brought hope and dignity to the world. But Procula is moved by the faith and compassion of her husband and she returns to his side.

Spark in Judea is a well-constructed play. The long years of apprenticeship for Delderfield were not wasted. Although the characters seem and sound more like British colonial officials and soldiers than Romans, nevertheless the dialogue is crisp, almost Shavian, and the well-researched plot moves with verve and conviction.

Two other plays by Delderfield saw experimental productions just prior to World War II: "Twilight Call" (1939), a comedy about the running of a garage, was produced by Barry Jackson's Repertory Theatre in Birmingham; and "Printer's Devil" (1939), a comedy about the workings of a small-town newspaper, was given a fringe-of-London tryout. "Printer's Devil" received additional productions, but both plays died with the advent of war and neither has been published.

In mid-war *This Is My Life* (1942) was produced in Wolverhampton under the title "Matron." The producer-director Basil Thomas coauthored the work. *This Is My Life* is set in a provincial hospital where the head nurse, Matron Jill Meddling, falls in love with Dr. Michael Britton, a crusading young physician fighting corruption and malpractice. He returns her love but she is faced with the choice between marriage and an important career of service. She chooses service over personal happiness. When her lover insists, "You ought to have a life of your own," she states her position: "This is my life."[2]

Dr. Britton is a character seemingly out of A. J. Cronin's *The Citadel* (1937), the popular exposé of pre–World War II medical abuses. Bert Trotter, a working-class patient who has beer smuggled in for him, provides comic relief and foreshadows Delderfield's working-class enlisted men in *Worm's Eye View* and later works. Confronted with his illegal drinking in bed, Trotter piously exclaims:

'Oo, what a wicked lie.

Britton: You better ask Dr. Garside if he won't lift the embargo.
Trotter: 'Oo says my embargo wants lifting? There's bin too much monkeyin' wiv my inside already. (*TIML*, 33)

This Is My Life is well-paced, witty, and authentic, indicating that Delderfield's long training as a playwright was bearing fruit. He had learned to write crisp, contemporary dialogue. What he needed was a viable and more substantial theme, and World War II provided it.

Postwar Success

When transferred out of Wolverhampton, Delderfield left a script with Basil Thomas and promptly forgot about its existence (*BEV*, 256). It was a comedy based on his negative experiences while billeted with civilians earlier in the war. Delderfield, along with many other British servicemen, felt abused and betrayed by the selfish, grasping, and inconsiderate civilians with whom they were temporarily ordered to live. He considered those who mistreated and cheated their own soldiers and airmen to be almost as evil as the Nazis. *Worm's Eye View* (1944), his most popular West End hit, was Delderfield's way of pointing out to the general public through satire the nature of the abuse. Delderfield was incommunicado on service in France and Belgium while Thomas, who had instantly realized that the topical play had great commercial possibilities, got together a production. After a provincial tour, *Worm's Eye View* made British theater history as the longest running play to its time.

The play is set in a civilian household at a seaside resort named Sandcombe and much like Morecambe, near Blackpool, where Delderfield had himself been billeted. In this well-made play the Bounty family has been required to billet several airmen, and they do so most ungraciously. Mrs. Bounty, ironically named, is no Lady Bountiful but rather an old battle-ax who henpecks her well-meaning but weak husband and tyrannizes the airmen. Her son by a prior marriage is the true villain of the piece as he attempts to break up the ingenuous love affair between his sister and Corporal Mark, the play's hero. The lovers prevail, of course, and the greedy civilians get their comeuppance, which delighted the wartime and postwar audiences, but the charm and vitality of the play does not reside in the love story but in the realistic, comic characterizations of the airmen in the billet. Delderfield drew his characters from life. Recruit Taffy, the radical ex–coal miner from Wales, was based on a clerk with whom Delderfield had served early in the war. His name was Taffy, too. He befriended Delderfield and the author repaid him with an admirable part in *Worm's Eye View* (*BEV*, 234–35). Pop, the old, retread airman, who plays cupid to Mark and Bella, was modeled on yet another military acquaintance who had helped Delderfield (*BEV*, 252).

However, Delderfield's finest character in the play is Porter, the hustling cockney, who fights the system successfully with persiflage and cunning for the aid and comfort of his buddies. Porter is one of Delderfield's most cogent comic inventions. The author liked his creation so much that he later reincarnated him as Pope the cockney in *Stop at a Winner* (1961). Cockney-born himself, Delderfield always had a warm spot in his heart and in his art for the inner-Londoner, the English equivalent to the streetwise New Yorker with the so-called Brooklyn accent.

Looking back on *Worm's Eye View* today, it is not easy to understand its popularity, although it is a charming comedy of human proportions. The key to the popularity that kept in on the stage from 1944 through 1951 is in timing. The play's success paralleled the revolt of the British public against Conservative party domination. Winston Churchill, who had led Britain throughout the war and who many called "The Man of the Century," was driven from office by a Socialist landslide in 1945 and both the Clement Atlee government and the welfare state took over.

The airmen in *Worm's Eye View* are fighting domination by the middle-class establishment much more than they are fighting the Germans. In fact, they are base troops, noncombatants. Their enemy is the system that allows their fellow countrymen, those with some money, to exploit, control, and abuse them. Delderfield, himself middle class and public-school educated, was no radical, but his British sense of justice and fair play gave birth to a cry for comity between the classes and power-sharing among all the people. He maintained this political position, essentially a liberal, but not radical one, throughout his literary career.

Meanwhile, the audiences, many of whom were mustered out servicemen and women, howled to see the antics of working-class enlisted men—grubby, grousing compatriots who washed their tired, dirty feet on the London stage—where before the war Noël Coward types played witty comedy in dinner dress. British comedy was never the same after Taffy the Welshman tries to make the best of the bad news that he and his buddy Porter the cockney have been posted to the Orkney Islands, saying, "Ah well, it might not be so bad. They say you can see the Northern Lights from the Orkneys"; to which Porter replies, "Don't talk daft mate, they got blackouts there same as everywhere else."[3] And when the villainous Sydney threatens to report the men to higher authority because they have tried to make themselves warm and to steal food withheld from them, Porter's astute response, "Watch out boys, he's goin' to appeal to 'Itler" (*WEV*, 72), touched everyone in the audience who had suffered at the hands of war profiteers, black market operators, and those who had abused and disdained the very men and women who had fought to preserve them and their way of life.

No Delderfield play ever came close to the acceptance and popularity of *Worm's Eye View*. "The Spinster of South Street" (1945), a play about the life of Florence Nightingale, was also touring but it was not successful and died before making it to a West End production. The play has not been published.

Peace Comes to Peckham (1946) deals with Anglo-American wartime and postwar understanding and misunderstanding in a light vein. A family in the working-class London suburb of Peckham, the Palfreys, have a son and daughter, Harry and Gloria, sent to America for safety during the war. After growing up in more peaceful and more prosperous conditions than they would have experienced at home, the two evacuees return to a Peckham reduced to a slum by bombings and postwar stringencies. Using cockney humor, contrasting British and American values, and family love, Delderfield shows how divided people may coalesce once more into a whole. Again Delderfield is excellent in portraying working-class characters, the lower middle class, and inner-Londoners, and again the plot is contrived and melodramatic. Nevertheless, it was well received by the London audiences if not all the critics, because once more Delderfield's timing was excellent. Thousands of children had returned from North America, and their readjustment problems needed airing in a gentle, humane, and good-natured way. The British themselves had to adjust to a younger generation, even those not evacuees, who wanted American wardrobes, who imitated American tastes and dialects in their music, and who became impatient with the scarred austerity of postwar Britain.

The characters in Delderfield's Peckham are war-groggy but resilient. The mother of the teenagers, Mrs. Palfrey, goes to great pains, literally and figuratively, to conceal from her children that she was wounded by a German bomb in the Blitz. Gloria's childhood sweetheart, Frank, has won the George Medal for bravery as a fireman. Her American sophistication and values do not sit well with her old beau, nor does Harry's American-style ambition appeal to his feckless father. To complicate matters further, Gloria's American boyfriend, Lieutenant Huck Kauffman, shows up to ask her to marry him but falls in love with her sister, Grace, who was not evacuated to America.

Naturally, the British get the best of it, and the audience is soothingly stroked, for Delderfield's Peckham is a warm, friendly locale, only superficially anti-American in fact. The sense of place is richly worked, and the reader is able to see in the drama the beginnings of Delderfield's first saga, *The Avenue* (1958).

In this early version of a Delderfield happy ending, kind hearts prevail, and the "dangers" of jitterbugging and chewing gum are put into a true perspective. As the play ends the cockney father, always nonplussed, hears his neighbor once more playing "There'll Always Be an England" on his annoying coronet. In total frustration at his inability to control events he shouts: "Orl right, orl right, we know there'll always be a perishin' England, but fer Gawd's sake don't rub it in."[4] Thus with a touch of flag-waving and resignation to an Americanized Britain, the curtain came down on Delderfield's second most successful comedy on the London stage.

All Over the Town (1947) is Delderfield's dramatization of his novel of the same name published the same year as the play was produced. It is set in a small seaside resort called Sandcombe—really Delderfield's Exmouth—and depicts the effects on a small, conservative, apathetic, hidebound community of a demobilized reformer,

Nat Hearn, a reporter on the *Sandcombe Clarion*, who finds himself
the editor of his old newspaper. Here is an opportunity to make
Sandcombe a better place to live. After all, if he had served his
country to make the world a better place to live in, why shouldn't he
try to do the same for his town? So, like Don Quixote, he sets off
with a vengeance to tilt at windmills. The villains opposing him
have the odds on their side. They range from a corrupt town councillor trying to push a bad housing project he has a financial interest in,
to a superannuated actress in community theater who does not care
for his scathing review of her ingenue role. In the end Hearn endures
and succeeds despite a strike and the breakdown of his press, for the
optimistic Delderfield is convinced that any English community can
become enlightened given the lead of a few good and dedicated
people. Facing a determined Saint George, the dragon of evil will
always deliquesce.

All Over the Town is a more credible play than *Peace Comes to
Peckham* in part because the author is dealing with a situation that is
nearly identical to the one he faced when he returned to the *Exmouth
Chronicle* from the R.A.F. The love story is plausible, the writing is
easy and competent, and the satire nonsavage. Once more Delderfield
addresses postwar problems, and he comes up with nonpartisan solu-
tions based on goodwill and good sense. Its popularity and the
expected happy denouement caused it to be the first Delderfield work
filmed. The movie was released in 1948.

The Queen Came By (1948) takes place in 1897 in the week of
Queen Victoria's Jubilee procession through London and in the staff
rooms of the Brixton branch of a chain department store. An older
milliner, Emmie, befriends seventeen-year-old Kitty who is having
an affair with a bounder named Albert. Kitty is loved by Roger, one
of the clerks, who is also a radical agitator for workers' rights. She
becomes pregnant by Albert, who is arrested for stealing on his job.
She attempts suicide, but Emmie and Roger pull her through despite
the opposition of callous, indifferent, and inhuman supervisors, managers, and employers. In the end, just before the Queen's procession
passes the store, Roger and Kitty recognize their mutual love and go
off to farm, while Emmie prepares to die of some unmentioned
disease.

Beyond placing the drama in time, the jubilee business has no
bearing, except that the store is competing in a window-dressing
competition. Delderfield, however, does re-create the Victorian mi-

lieu in the attitudes and values of his characters. Unfortunately, the play is meretriciously sentimental melodrama filled with stereotypical situations and characters who are ineluctably drawn to obvious conclusions. *The Queen Came By* seems to have been an early work of Delderfield, dusted off and produced to cash in on his name and on the success of *Worm's Eye View*, which was still going strong in the West End. Although well made and structurally taut, the play has only one interesting and original character, Ridge, the cockney janitor, whose salty language and disdain for his superiors provide a refreshing contrast to the cliché-ridden speeches of the others, such as Kitty's dream: "I think I'll have a house in the country with bow windows and a balcony hanging with flowers like the pictures on the cover of our Travelwear Catalogue this month."⁵

Despite the play's shortcomings, however, it was moved from the fringe theater where it was first performed, to a West End house, the Duke of York's Theatre, where it had a respectable run. The London audience was happy with Delderfield's drama. After the ordeal of the war many wanted light, diverting plays, melodramas, and simple comedies with satisfying, happy endings. However, as the 1940s ended the taste of that audience began to shift, and Delderfield either was unable to or chose not to adapt to the new interests.

Plays of the Fifties: The String Running Out

Delderfield decided to write a sequel to *Bird's Eye View* in the hope that there was more mileage to be gotten out of his cockney and Welsh vagabond ex-airmen. *Waggonload o' Monkeys: Further Adventures of Porter and Taffy* (1951) finds Porter using Taffy to help him turn a down and out country pub into a marketable property. Delderfield does not build Porter as strikingly resourceful as he needed to in order to make this a hilarious play, but the scheme to dress up an amorous, buxom barmaid as the headless horror of local fame so that Porter can drum up business is clever, and the ever sanctimonious Taffy, caught up a chimney in a suit of armor, provides many laughs. Delderfield, who wasted little and recycled much of his experience, used this incident again ten years later in *Stop at a Winner*.

The weakness of *Waggonload o' Monkeys* is that far too much time is spent in setting up the farcical situation, and thus the resolution seems an anticlimax. Nevertheless, Delderfield turns out excellent comic dialogue, such as when Porter's London girlfriend shows up in Devon and says: "But Sam, we been separated for months an' yo 'aven't even kissed me." Porter replies: "Sex! That's all you women think of, what is Sex."[6]

The comedy *Golden Rain* (1952) was produced in Windsor but did not achieve a West End production. It is the story of a young, provincial minister, Roger Strawbridge, and his spirited wife Cathy. They are saddled with a deteriorating rectory, and Cathy tries various ways, some less than appropriate for a cleric's wife, to obtain funds to improve their lives. She even tries to sell off the rectory to a credulous "Yank" Mrs. Stukely-Mosher; "a crank o' course," says the comic housekeeper, "but you'd expect 'er to be, wouldn't you, what with bein' a Yank *and* pokin' about other people's 'ouses just because they 'ad dry rot in 'em."[7] Success in the football pools only embarrasses the poor rector, who spends much of his time lecturing not only his parish but also his wife on ethical behavior. Finally, Cathy learns to accept her lot, and the good minister can return to guiding his flock.

Golden Rain is a gentle comedy that relies on fairly obvious and inconsequential parish incidents for its limited humor. Its episodal structure reads much like a pilot for a television sitcom. The bite had gone out of Delderfield's comedy. He was no longer using comic situations to satirize human foibles or social problems in a significant way.

The Offending Hand (1953) was produced in Northampton but never made it to the West End. The play's subject is the indulgent treatment of criminals in the welfare state. Kenneth Lowrey, a bad seed youth, hurts all the members of his family as he proceeds from one crime to another. Finally, his sister, with gun in hand, forces him to turn himself in. The play is a melodrama and the characters tend to caricature: a mollycoddling aunt, a widower schoolmaster father, a sister whose fiancé is the arresting policeman, and a doting girlfriend. Delderfield's strong criticism of the British justice system is the reverse of John Galsworthy's pleas in *Justice* (1910) for more humane treatment of young criminals. Jean, the sister so ready to cut off "the offending hand," sounds like someone speaking in the 1980s rather than the 1950s when she addresses her policeman beau: "I'll tell you what you should do—clamp down on people like Ken right from the start, instead of wrapping him up in your paraphernalia of special courts and probation officers and come-come-let's-talk-it-over twaddle."[8] Given the ultraliberal political tenor of the time, it is not surprising that *The Offending Hand* did not attract a London producer.

The next play of Delderfield to reach London's West End after provincial tryouts was *The Orchard Walls* (1953). Beginning with *The Offending Hand*, it was Delderfield's unfulfilled intention to write a series of "social problem" plays (*BEV*, 264). *Worm's Eye View* had finally closed. No other play of his had been a major success. He needed a hit production to keep his name and his work before the theatergoing public. As he finished writing his first autobiography, *Bird's Eye View* (1954), he wondered about *The Orchard Walls*: "Perhaps its fate will shape my future output so that this journal ends, as it began, on a note of query" (*BEV*, 264). It did. *The Orchard Walls*, an honest, good-hearted play about education and adolescent love, two of Delderfield's favorite subjects, is a serious drama about serious subjects not often dealt with on the English stage to that time, but it is also a lightweight drama with an obvious solution to a stock confrontation between the enlightened and sympathetic headmistress of a girls' school in a cathedral town and the socialite mother of the teenage heroine.

As usual in a Delderfield play, characterization is strong, and the plot, this one neatly spanning a forty-eight-hour period, is tight. The headmistress has personal problems of her own, the controlling mother is credible, and the local editor, who is on the school board, is drawn from life. But Delderfield was unable or unwilling to grapple with the major social and political problems of his time. He saw drama in almost a nineteenth-century way: cleverly crafted entertainment, provoking a modicum of thought and a bundle of feeling, leaving the audience well satisfied with a pat solution. Unlike Shaw or Galsworthy he chose craftsmanship over discussion in depth. He valued the well-made play over the ragged problem. Those factors eliminate Delderfield's serious plays from ultimate consideration as a part of the mainstream of British drama.

In *The Orchard Walls* Delderfield might have slammed the pettiness, sexual hypocrisy, and class rigidity of small-town life that nearly drives a young girl to suicide; or he could have attacked the public (private) school system that perpetuates a class- and sex-segregated society: the play's plot offered both opportunities. But he did not; instead, he rejected an appeal to reform and chose to stand behind the values of the school system he evolved from and the community he lived in so comfortably. The result is yet another well-made and entertaining drama that leaves the playgoer with a pleasant glow and not much else to think about except some supper.

The Orchard Walls had a respectful reception, but it surely became clear to theater managers and producers as well as to Delderfield himself that he had little to say that would stimulate critical or intellectual discussion in a theater now receptive to such plays as T. S. Eliot's The Cocktail Party (1949) and The Confidential Clerk (1953), Graham Greene's The Living Room (1953), and Samuel Beckett's Waiting for Godot (1953). As the play passed to oblivion, however, Delderfield salvaged the romantic plot of young lovers humiliated and torn apart by the selfish, snobbish mother of the girl, and used it for the basis for his novel, There Was a Fair Maid Dwelling (1960), the first part of the Diana saga.

Where There's a Will (1953) had a fringe theater run and then opened in the West End in 1954. It is a comedy based on the clash of values between Londoners and country folk. An old Devonshire farmer dies apparently intestate. His cockney relatives descend on the run-down farm to claim it. They are a grasping lot except for the farmer's middle-aged bachelor nephew, Alfie, who has always wanted to be a farmer but for reasons not clear in the play has never tried farming, although he has taken a home-study course in agriculture and has also had success growing asparagus on a plot in the city. Also an exception to the surly group is Alfie's niece June, who falls in love with a local farmer and must decide between returning to London life or staying on in Devon.

Of course, Alfie, who is now enamored with the farm and who himself is the object of the affections of Annie, the deceased farmer's 36-year-old housekeeper, succeeds in getting her to stay. He argues that in London she would have to "rush fer the perishin' tube night an' mornin'; fight yer way through ten thahsand other mugs fer a cup o' stood tea an' a rock-cake lunchtime; choke yerself ter death wi' petrol exhaust. . . ."⁹ She stays of course. Alfie has more trouble in keeping the farm, but finally wins out over his treacherous brother-in-law, Fred. It turns out that Annie is the real heir after all, and she and Alfie will inherit, marry, and live happily ever after.

Where There's a Will is pretty thin comedy although the play has a pleasant glow about it. From the beginning the audience expects that the bachelor and the spinster will marry and that Alfie will achieve his dream of farming. The plot merely exists to hang one good character on—Alfie—but even he becomes difficult to accept when he begins to wax rhapsodic about country life: "you've on'y got to take a bunch of Britishers from offices an' factories an' put 'em in a boat and push off, and in no time at all they're first-class sailors; they don't 'have to learn, they sort of know it all. It's the same wi' the land. We ain't reely city folk, none of us. 'Ardly any time ago, before they started running up fact'ry chimneys all over the auction, the whole perishin' lot of us was livin' orf the land" (*WTAW*, 58).

The poetic Alfie is unbelievable and even embarrassing. There is not enough edge or bite in the play. Delderfield confines his artistic goals here to the entertainment level of ordinary television comedy. Essentially, Delderfield is repeating the *Worm's Eye View* formula: a minor love intrigue set against the background of regional or class conflict with obvious reconciliation the denouement.

Uncle's Little Lapse (published in 1955) is a farce written for amateur theater groups. *The Mayerling Affair* (1957) was produced at the Pitlochry Festival after a BBC-TV production the previous year. It is Delderfield's first three-act historical drama and is based on one of the most dramatic single events in nineteenth-century European history, the joint suicide of the heir to the throne of Austria-Hungary, Archduke Rudolph, and his mistress, Baroness Maria Vetsera, in 1889, at the Royal Hunting Lodge in the village of Mayerling.

Delderfield's Rudolph is a weak-willed, morphine-addicted liberal in whose shaky hands lay the hopes of democrats in Austria who wish to break the autocratic power of the Hapsburgs, a power which, allied with the Prussians under Bismarck and the kaisers, could and did lead to the cataclsym of World War I. Rudolph's supporters believe that without him "The Concert of Europe will dissolve into two armed camps, with loaded cannon trained on each other awaiting only some further folly . . . to plunge every European into a machine-made hell."[10] They also rightly fear that all his promise and potential could be "thrown aside by the thrust of a girl's hips" (*MA*, 58). The thirty-year-old libertine prince, married to the hectoring and self-pitying Princess Stephanie, has fallen deeply in love with a nineteen-year-old beauty, and he, like Britain's Edward VIII, would prefer to divorce his wife and marry his Mary rather than save Europe. Ranged against the handsome, charming, but degenerate prince and his brave and beautiful lover are all the forces of the empire, personified by Rudolph's father, Emperor Franz Joseph. In the end their enemies prove too strong, Mary takes her own life, and Rudolph follows her action to be with her in death.

The Mayerling Affair is rich and satisfying historical drama.

Delderfield is almost always at his best when he can call on his historical research. The setting is totally believable, and there is nothing of *The Student Prince* or *The Prisoner of Zenda* in either plot or characterization. In the best Greek tradition the play is both history and tragedy complete with an authentic, flawed tragic hero and the strong presence of fate and destiny. Perhaps if *The Mayerling Affair* had not first found a large television audience, it would have provided the medium for a Delderfield comeback in the West End.

In *Flashpoint* (published in 1958) Delderfield finally accomplishes what he set out to do when he wrote *The Orchard Walls*: write a successful problem play (*BEV*, 264). *Flashpoint* deals passionately and intelligently with the post–World War II conflict between wealthy landowners who were trying to preserve the countryside from the encroachment of cancerous, massive development, and the liberal social planners who were trying to make the limited physical resources of the nation available to most of the public.

Lady Edith Breconridge has lost her husband in World War I and three of her four sons in World War II and later skirmishes. She wants her surviving son, Keith, to leave school teaching and return to the family estate, which she is struggling mightily to restore. She hopes that Keith will succeed her and continue the way of life she cherishes. In trying to realize her dream of restoration of place and milieu she runs roughshod over people: those who have been renting from her, and even Keith, who has surprised her by bringing home a fiancée, a widow with a daughter.

Janet Grimshaw, the widow, claims that her husband died in the war. Lady Edith is suspicious and has the claim secretly investigated behind the couple's back. It turns out that Janet's husband did not die in battle as claimed, but, as she well knew, was a murderer whom she shielded and who later died accidentally. When the play ends, Janet is under suspicion as an accessory to murder; there is doubt that the love, based on lies, will survive the coming ordeal; and Keith is estranged from his mother forever. Everyone has lost. The best of plans have turned to dust because of distrust and blind determination.

Flashpoint is both subtle and powerful. The play is reminiscent of John Galsworthy's problem plays like *Strife* (1909) and *Loyalties* (1922). Following Galsworthy's typical plan, a problem is posed, both sides are presented, and it turns out that there is right and wrong in both camps. Furthermore, headstrong antagonists complicate the issues with their personal, often selfish agendas. One sympa-thizes with Lady Edith, who is "sixty-eight, and she's lived to see all the people she cared about killed, and scattered, or packed into two-roomed flatlets. Out of the entire bunch of them, she's survived, largely on account of her own brains and guts."[11]

Keith, who is a reasonable and decent young man, must finally oppose his mother and her dreams because she proceeds from and presumes an unmitigated authoritarian position. He says: "You planners—Right, Left and Centre—oh. God, you're so blind—you've got faith in yourselves and hope in your blueprints—your mistake is that all of your shut out charity and sooner or later everything you touch goes sour. What a poor, shabby thing tradition becomes when it turns its back on pity" (*F*, 71).

This fine, emotional speech reflects Delderfield's old-fashioned, almost Edwardian Liberal, view—a view far from acceptable in the polarized post–World War II British society. That unfashionableness, and the Galsworthian technique of emphasizing the questions with-out providing pat, philosophical or theatrical answers, may explain why the play, richly crafted like a novel, and Delderfield's finest serious drama to the time, did not find a producer and a West End run. It should have. Alas, by the late 1950s it appears that the London audience had lost interest in Delderfield, or thought of him only as a farceur.

Last Plays

Once Aboard the Lugger (1962) was first presented in Plymouth by the Exmouth Players, Delderfield's hometown amateur theater soci-ety. The pleasant and satisfying comedy focuses on the character of the native Devonshireman, and in that sense is reminiscent of the novels *All Over the Town* (1947), *Farewell, the Tranquil Mind* (1950), and *There Was a Fair Maid Dwelling* (1960).

Walter Pearcey is a Devon sailor, secretly in love with Molly Drayton, who finds a sunken treasure of gold coins. He shares news of the find with Molly's officious brother, a man unappreciative of his sister's contribution to his domestic well-being.

Walter wants to take Molly and her daughter away with him on his boat to live out their lives far from the welfare state. In the end he cleverly manages to keep his treasure despite the best efforts of the

government and Molly's relatives, and the little family-to-be sails
away for the Greek isles.

Delderfield takes the opportunity in *Once Aboard the Lugger* to get
in another swipe at big government when he has Walter note that "it
gets worse instead o' better every day. We turned so many ole corners
since the war we must be spinning like a whip top—cost o' living
rocketing, officials of one sort and another plaguing the life out of all
of us, wars and revolutions everywhere, and people hauled off to
clink for saying we don't want to be blowed sky-high by the
bomb."[12]

Once Aboard the Lugger has several improbabilities in the plot. Also,
the audience is expected to sympathize with a man who is in fact
breaking the law of treasure trove and stealing what belongs to the
state. Still, the humor is sharp, one-liners abound, and Delderfield's
characters are broadly stroked, leaving no doubt as to who is good
and who is bad. However, the play remained in the amateur theater
canon.

"My Dearest Angel"(1963), Delderfield's last play, was successfully
produced at the Pitlochry Festival but, unlike *The Mayerling Affair*,
has not been published. Delderfield's career as a playwright simply
spluttered out as he lost interest in the professional theater. He spent
some twenty-five or more years writing plays. None of them, not
even *Worm's Eye View*, will be long remembered or become a part of
the permanent English repertory. Still, writing plays prepared him
for his role as a novelist in that it trained him to think in dramatic
terms, to value plots, to remember that if, as Aristotle says, a play is
an action, then how much better a historical novel would be if it too
is an action.

Delderfield did make one contribution to the English stage that is
of some significance. In *Worm's Eye View* he introduced working-class
characters who were central to the play and not merely servants or
part of the comic relief. A more affluent English working-class audience could now comfortably join the traditional middle-class theater
audience in seeing themselves favorably, respectfully, and centrally
portrayed on the stage. Future histories of the English stage will
probably not link Delderfield to Joe Orton's *What the Butler Saw*
(1969) or David Storey's *The Contractor* (1970); nevertheless, the
realism and the absurdist comedy of the late modern and postmodern
British theater derived from the changes brought to the stage by
those war veteran writers like Delderfield who broke away with a

vengeance from the drawing-room comedy and upper-class drama of the prewar period.

One-Act Plays

Although Delderfield made fun of amateur theater societies in his novels, he enjoyed writing one-act plays for them. In all he wrote fifteen short plays for drama groups. Many were written in the 1930s and 1940s but all were published between 1952 and 1962. In fact, thirteen of his one-act dramas were published between 1952 and 1955, when, of course, he was at the height of his fame as a playwright.

Among the more outstanding short plays are *Sailors Beware* (1950),[13] a delightful historical farce in which Elizabeth I insures a swift victory over the Spanish Armanda by advising her officers that their wives will be spending their money in London until they return; *The Old Lady of Cheadle* (1952), a historical comedy set in 1745 at the time of the brief return to Britain of Bonnie Prince Charlie; *The Testimonial* (1953), in which a couple celebrating their fifty years of marriage privately reveal the sacrifices each has made to keep the marriage intact; *The Bride Wore an Opal Ring* (1952), a domestic comedy about a premarital crisis in which the bride finally realizes that she is marrying the wrong man and instead runs off with her ex-lover, the journalist covering the wedding; *The Rounderlay Tradition* (1954), an all-woman comedy in which the seventeenth-century Rounderlay family ghost prevents her twentieth-century descendant from choosing the wrong husband; *Ten till Five* (1954), a fluffy office comedy in which a plain-looking secretary longs for her handsome but indifferent boss until she learns the secret of allure from a Frenchwoman; *Home Is the Hunted* (1954), a cockney comedy in which a London criminal who has momentarily escaped from the police is driven to give himself up because of the bickering of his fractious family as they argue over hiding places for him; *The Guinea-Pigs* (1954), in which a woman's church delegation calls on a wealthy possible benefactress who uses them as guinea pigs for her terrible "gourmet" cooking; and *Wild Mink* (1962), an office comedy about a cockney used-car dealer who is trapped into giving his wife the mink coat he bought from a crooked furrier instead of giving it to his mistress-secretary.

Delderfield's one-act plays were a labor of love. He realized that

their commercial possibilities were limited to a few pounds in royal-
ties from amateur productions. He wrote them because he was genuinely fond of community theaters. He respected their integrity and
their amateurness in the best sense of that word, the shared love of
an art form. However, his efforts in this minor genre also helped him
to sharpen characterization so that Delderfield dramatic characters in
his three-act plays are presented strongly and clearly from their first
moment on the stage. Furthermore, the one-acters provided exercises
in concision. Delderfield's full-length plays are always taut. There is
never a sense of marking time in them. That quality of construction
came from the discipline demanded by the one-act play.

It may be that there will one day be a revival of interest in the
performance of one-act plays, as has been the case with the return of
the short story in the late 1970s and 1980s. If so, evenings of
Delderfield's short comedies may become as much a staple of little
theater productions as the three-act comedies of Alan Ayckbourn are
today.

Delderfield the playwright was a careful craftsman who employed
clearly defined characters, often types, in credible situations. He
sought to entertain first and educate second. His essential optimism
and cheerfulness helped brighten a postwar Britain still suffering
from personal losses, emotional strains, and economic distress. He
found and met a need in his audience for rueful laughter, salving
pride, and emerging hope.

Chapter Three
Achieving the Tranquil Mind: First Novels

R. F. Delderfield began to write fiction shortly after his success with *Worm's Eye View*. At first fiction was a corollary to his work as a dramatist, but as successes in the theater diminished and his dislike for the medium and its practitioners grew, he found greater and greater satisfaction, control, and success with the novel form. Three novels mark his apprenticeship: *All Over the Town* (1947), *Seven Men of Gascony* (1949), and *Farewell, the Tranquil Mind* (1950). Carefully and wisely, he began his efforts in the novel by keeping to subjects and locales he knew well: small-town life and journalism, and French Revolutionary and Napoleonic history, the latter his favorite reading.

All Over the Town

Delderfield's first long work of fiction is a version of his play by the same name and thus is constructed in taut dramatic form. In it the hero, returning serviceman Nat Hearn, undertakes a journalistic quest to right three wrongs in his home town of Sandcombe. All three incidents are resolved in a satisfactory manner, and the hero wins the hand of the attractive reporter who has replaced him while he was on active service in World War II.

All Over the Town is a novel in the manner of a well-made play, and
this statement is by no means meant to be a derogatory one, for the
structure of the novel benefits greatly from Delderfield's ability and
experience as a dramatist: the action takes place within a very few
weeks, characters are strongly drawn, and the hero's triumph and the
novel's resolution are extremely satisfying. If the denouement appears
obvious almost from the beginning and if it is quite clear from early
on that Mollie the girl reporter has had little to do in life except wait
in the wings for Nat, still the reader is quite satisfied at the end of
the book, satisfied in a way not at all dissimilar from the way he or
she is satisfied when the curtain comes down on a Delderfield play.

Furthermore, the atmosphere of a small Devonshire seaside resort
town is created so finely that one can only admire Delderfield's
observational skills and his courage in obviously caricaturing not only
the community in which he had resided for twenty-four years but
also some of his relatives and many of his friends and neighbors. The
newspaper Nat Hearn works for, the *Sandcombe Clarion*, is owned by a
hypocritical, miserly, but well-meaning curmudgeon named Sam
Vane, clearly modeled after Delderfield's father, who was the owner of
the *Exmouth Chronicle*. Sam's son, Gerald, the insecure, snobbish, and
mealy mouthed printer who inherits the rickety weekly after Sam's
death and who invites Nat to buy into a partnership and edit the
paper, is fashioned after Delderfield's printer brother, Eric. Although
neither man is painted black, still the portraits are far from compli-
mentary. Furthermore, one senses from the portraits of Miss Gelding,
the vainglorious, self-consecrated but superannuated star of the Sandcombe Amateur Operatic Society; Town Councillor Baines, the crafty
demagogue trying to get the community to build a housing project
far enough out of town so that he can make a killing with his bus
line; Major Matindale, M.C., so conservative and self-interested that
he will cotton no change in the community that might affect its
quaintness; the Reverend Galahad Ormsby, the wishy-washy minister
who is manipulated by a conniving churchwarden into trying to
divert funds from a legacy for a memorial to the war dead to the
obtaining of a new church organ for a parish church that no ex-
serviceman or -woman attends; and the besotted writer Otto de Vere,
"one of Sandcombe's proudest possessions," who "earned what was
considered to be a fabulous income by writing thrillers and who lived
in sin with a somewhat raddled blonde in a big house on the edge of
the cliff"[1] that these characters are all based on Exmouth acquaintances of the author.

As editor of the *Sandcombe Clarion*, and with his pusillanimous partner out of town, Nat attempts to purge the amateur opera society of strangling leadership, reform the corrupt town council, and chastise the local Anglican church council. Naturally he runs into opposition and counterattacks, and even Mollie leaves him temporarily, peeved because he chauvinistically neglected to inform her, his fiancée, that he was putting his life savings and their future into the paper. But Nat is undaunted in his belief that creating a better Britain must begin in small places and in small ways.

However, Gerald leads a strike of the pressmen against Nat. The corrupt or selfish members of the community whom Nat has attacked in his editorials respond to him by cutting their advertising in the *Clarion*. The printing press itself breaks down and Nat is near to despair and defeat when Mollie returns to help him, decent townsfolk rally to his support, the pressmen prove that they love their ancient newspaper more than the promise of a future raise, and even Gerald realizes that Nat's moral stance is correct and must be supported at least to a point. Mollie and Nat will marry and the *Clarion* will evolve as a real newspaper, not merely a collection of advertisements and wedding and funeral announcements.

All Over the Town is so amiable a book that it is difficult not to smile automatically in recalling it. Nat Hearn, the tall, rumpled, easygoing, but highly principled protagonist reminds one of the hero in an early James Stewart movie like "Mr. Smith Goes to Washington." One knows from the beginning that the forces of good cannot remain long defeated and they will rally round the hero. The good guys and girls are clearly destined to win, and the bad guys—one should probably say "chaps" with Delderfield—are really not all that bad. The battles won, Nat "went over to kiss the top of her (Mollie's) head, and she squeezed his hand" (*AOTT*, 191). Then they made tea and "Sandcombe came alive again" (*AOTT*, 192).

Today *All Over the Town* reads as a delightful piece of nostalgia, a picture of the England that millions of servicemen dreamed about returning to after the war. Sandcombe is an ideal. It never was, nor never could be, but oh, if it were possible.

Seven Men of Gascony

Seven Men of Gascony is a strikingly different novel from *All Over the Town* and much more like its successor, *Farewell, the Tranquil Mind*. Both *Seven Men of Gascony* and *Farewell, the Tranquil Mind* are historical novels based on Delderfield's passionate interest in, and study of, French history in the Revolutionary and Napoleonic periods. *Seven Men of Gascony* is a vivid work, full of flaming battle scenes, glorious victories, and monumental routs. The story is the remembrance of an old veteran of the Napoleonic Wars, an artist named Gabriel, who recalls the events of his service as he dies twenty-five years after the Battle of Waterloo.

The seven men are all enlisted men in Napoleon's infantry. They are the GIs, the Tommies, the Grunts of their time. They serve in the Eighty-Seventh Regiment of the line as *voltigeurs*, light infantry used by Napoleon as front line sharpshooters to draw enemy fire so that the heavy troops behind them could judge the enemy's positions. The life expectancy of a *voltigeur* in battle is very short indeed, and the reason that these Gascons survive as long as they do is that they are led by wily old Sergeant Jean, a veteran of Italy, Egypt, Marengo, Austerlitz, Jena, Eylau, and Friendland. As the inner story opens and Gabriel joins the file, it is May 1809 and the regiment is positioned on an island in the Danube just before a battle. Sergeant Jean Ticquet, father-surrogate to his boy soldiers, who seems based on the nearly immortal veteran, Stanislaus Katczinsky, in Erich Maria Remarque's *All Quiet on the Western Front* (1928), is determined that his recruits will not be decimated.

The other squad members are Manny, the handsome, romantic Jew; Claude, the idealistic young revolutionist; Louis, the lover of horses; Nicholas, the scholar; and Dominique, the fiddle-playing, slow-thinking, farm boy. The Grand Army of Napoleon is temporarily enjoying its last unchecked sweep across the map of Europe. In the subsequent campaigns the Gascons will be picked off slowly, one by one, during the next five years in Austria, the Iberian Peninsula, Russia, Germany, and France. Sergeant Jean will die at Waterloo along with the last hopes of the emperor. Gabriel, of course, survives, although his hand is mutilated. He inherits the beautiful and high-spirited *cantinière,* Nicholette, who has followed the regiment and particularly Jean's squad, from Austria to Moscow to Spain to France and to Waterloo, with her canteen wagon, like Brecht's Mother Courage, replacing husbands from the file.

In *Seven Men of Gascony* Delderfield felicitously begins his first historical novel with the premise that men and women in past generations were pretty much like ourselves: the soldiers complain about everything from chow to stupid decisions by their officers.

Still, Delderfield shows us how hundreds of thousands of young men could have endured every trial and face near certain death or mutilation for Napoleon and the instrument of destiny he forged: the Grand Army. The soldiers seek more food, dry quarters, occasional lovemaking, and a chance to survive. The women, particularly Nicholette, are strong, independent, resolute, and assertive in sexual decisions. As an ex-serviceman himself, one who led a unit of men moving through France and Belgium in wartime while living off the land, Delderfield knew that few things in life bind men closer to each other than combat. Men, and in this case women, who share the privations of campaigning, the long marches, captivity, escape, victory, defeat, and death are brothers and sisters for all eternity. The survivor, in this instance Gabriel, lives out his life with the feeling of incompleteness, as if the anticlimax of a peaceful middle and old age is merely a soldier's long wait to join his comrades in the line. As Gabriel dies:

A great joy flooded his heart. He began to run, calling the men's names one after the other, until they ceased chattering among themselves and began to shout back at him and to wave their hands.

Although the wagon did not seem to be moving at more than a walking pace, it proved extraordinarily difficult to catch; but the veteran made every effort . . . coming a little nearer with each stride and reaching out to touch the hands of the men that were stretched towards him.

At last, with an immense feeling of relief, he drew near enough to be grabbed by the wrist and pulled into the wagon. The six men squeezed together to make room for him on the crowded tailboard. They shouted and laughed, thumping him between the shoulders. Even in the excitement of the moment Gabriel could not help noticing that the fingers of his hand were straight again and that the palm no longer showed a puckered scar.

The speed of the wagon increased as somewhere in front of them, a girl's voice shouted, "Hup, hup!" to the plodding horse.[2]

Delderfield's vivid prose drips blood and reeks with the smell of war. Brutality is rampant. Naturally decent men both face and commit horrors, and corpses pile up by the tens of thousands as a continent destroys itself in seemingly unending conflict.

The novel is structured on the fate of the men in the file. Manny is the first of the seven to die, crucified by Spanish guerrillas. Claude drowns in the Tagus River. Louis, now a cavalryman, is murdered for his horse's flesh by starving French troops in the terrible retreat from

Moscow. Nicholas is shot for desertion after the Battle of Lützen. Dominique is mortally injured by a horse's hooves while retreating across a river after the defeat at Leipzig. Old Sergeant Jean dies in the last battle, Waterloo, and Gabriel is left to remember.

Of the many battle scenes superbly described, Waterloo stands out for minute precision and clarity:

Now that La Haye Sainte was in French hands the British gunners on the ridge had opened fire once more and the shots were flailing down on the shattered buildings, splintering tiles, pitting the cob walls of the farm and sending out spurts of choking dust. The battalion poured from the yard, fanned out in the field between farm and plateau, and advanced in skirmishing order, kneeling, firing and loading, closing in on the emplacements, where little red figures crouched and ran, sponged, sighted and died. (*SM*, 342)

Of course there are lulls in the fighting. In one Gabriel meets an Austrian girl and he plans to leave the army and marry her, but she dies in a fire, and he realizes that the army is his destiny. When the squad is captured and sent to England a noblewoman falls in love with Louis and nearly kills her jealous husband over him. She then helps the Gascons to escape by boat. This episode is the only unbelievable section in the novel, for not only is *Seven Men of Gascony* an outstanding example of its genre, the war story, it is an exemplar of verisimilitude. Delderfield never wrote better historical fiction.

Farewell, the Tranquil Mind

Farewell, the Tranquil Mind, the last novel in Delderfield's experimental early period, is the second of three historical war romances, the third being *Too Few For Drums* (1964). Of the three it is the least successful, possibly because it is not based on events of the Napoleonic Wars as are *Seven Men of Gascony* and *Too Few for Drums*, but on the French Revolutionary period of which Delderfield knew somewhat less, although the author clearly researched the period thoroughly for the book. It is simply that neither person, place, nor event ring true in this work as they do in *Seven Men of Gascony*. Also, unlike *Seven Men of Gascony* and *Too Few for Drums*, Delderfield seems to be stuffing and tucking history into odd corners of the novel as if he were trying to tell both the story of the entire French Revolution and the story of a Devonshire farm lad, David Treloar, at the same time. For example, Delderfield has an ignorant French bargeman give a sophisticated account of the politics of the Revolution.[3] Even more improbably, he has a peasant counterrevolutionary soldier explain why he is a resistance fighter in a seemingly lost cause, and in doing so sound like a political scientist: "The squat Vendéan rose and stretched himself. 'You ask an eternal question, M'sieur Treloar,' he replied. 'Why did your Kentish peasants march against Feudalism under Tyler and Cade? Why did the followers of Johan Huss offer themselves up as martyrs for a page or two of Dogma? Why do the redskins of America continually sacrifice their lives in a hopeless effort to confine the white colonist to his coastal strip?'"(*FTM*, 292).

Telling the story of the French Revolution and the high adventures of David Treloar and the French girl he marries, Charlotte Lamotte, makes for a great deal of plot, some of it hard to accept. The events of the novel, which purportedly are a version of his account written in prison and revised by David's grandson, take place between spring 1792 and January 1794. David is a twenty-year-old farmer whose father is head of a Devon smuggling ring. In the course of an attempt to land contraband goods from France, the father and all of David's brothers are killed because David's mother has chosen to betray them in order to save the farm for David. The mother hoped that her husband and sons would be captured and lightly punished but her plans go awry. In anger she kills the leader of the exicisemen and is killed herself as her farm burns to the ground. Sure to be implicated, the innocent David runs for his life; is aided by a secret Whig sympathizer and friend of Tom Paine, author of *Common Sense* and *The Rights of Man*; and escapes to Revolutionary France where he quickly learns that the Revolution has certainly not created a just democracy.

In Paris he is befriended by André, a cynical medical student, and taken to live with André's family, where he meets Charlotte. Quite improbably, David gets caught up in the turmoils of the Revolution as it evolves from idealism to violence and then to uncontrolled savagery. Delderfield sketches the major figures of the Revolution: Paine, for whom David has become a translator, Robespierre, Brissot, Marat, and Danton, and he presents group portraits of the Convention, the Committee of Safety, the National Guard, in which David and André serve, and the brutal Mob. The reader witnesses through David's eyes the storming of the Tuileries, the guillotining of King Louis XVI, and the suffering of Queen Marie Antoinette.

Finally, David and Charlotte must flee for their lives after David rescues his wife from the clutches of the seducer Dr. Gemaine, head of the insane asylum in which she and her relatives have taken refuge to escape the guillotine. Charlotte kills the doctor who has defiled her and David also does his share of killing, including a vicious general in the Revolutionary army. Their goal is America where they hope to farm. However, the American ship that is taking them to the New World is stopped by a British warship and the young couple, now married, are brought to England where David is put into prison awaiting trial for his supposed part in the death of the exciseman. The ending is deus ex machina. Charlotte, who knows very little English and who has almost no money, is nevertheless able to convince the Admiralty to arrange a pardon for David in exchange for some military papers he took off the person of the murdered general and which for some unexplained reason Charlotte has been carrying around for months. Of course, the young couple end up on the restored family farm in Devon to live happily ever after.

Despite the high adventures and the excellent historical descriptions, *Farewell, the Tranquil Mind* seldom seems to come to life. This is due not only to Delderfield's attempt to stuff too much history into the novel but also to the blandness of both hero and heroine. David, a stereotypically cold English fish, hardly ever gets excited about the momentous events occurring about him, and he does not even realize when a comely young woman is expressing her deep feelings for him.

Farewell, the Tranquil Mind has a political moral: the center cannot hold; it does not pay to be a moderate reformer in a revolution that is bent on violence, for the fall will come sooner rather than later. Delderfield holds up for emulation Britain's constitutional monarchy which evolved from the almost bloodless Glorious Revolution of 1688. Delderfield would have liked to have seen the French copy their British neighbors. A constitutional monarchy would have avoided, he believed, the excesses of the Revolution and even the misery dealt Europe after Napoleon's coup d'état.

All Over the Town, Seven Men of Gascony, and *Farewell, the Tranquil Mind*, although by no means best-sellers, were critically and financially successful enough to encourage Delderfield to continue writing novels. He knew he could create viable fictional characters; he realized that he had skill in description; he saw that he could blend historical fact with archetypal human actions in a credible way. Now he needed to find themes and milieus closer to home and more profound.

Chapter Four
The Early Sagas

R. F. Delderfield's first two sagas spanned the three experiences he drew upon continually for story and drama: the life of suburban London, West Country life in seaside Devon, and military service in World War II. *The Avenue Story*, which was first published in two parts in 1958, *The Dreaming Suburb*, and *The Avenue Goes to War*; and *Diana*, which was also originally published in two parts: *There Was a Fair Maid Dwelling* (1960), and its sequel, *The Unjust Skies* (1962), are the books that commenced Delderfield's march to international renown as a novelist. They came at a brief equipoise in his writing career as his interest in and success with writing plays was waning and his appreciation for the novelist's control of his medium was waxing. The artistic success of *The Avenue Story*, in that he proved to himself that he could juggle the stories of several families in various locales simultaneously in the grand Russian manner of Tolstoy, and the commercial success of *Diana*, which proved to Delderfield that he could achieve with the novel the kind of international recognition he had failed to obtain with the play, tipped the balance, and Delderfield the novelist replaced Delderfield the dramatist.

The Avenue Story

The Avenue Story is Delderfield's saga of the suburbs in peace and war, the story of five families, some twenty people who live on Manor Park Avenue, a suburban street outside of London and bordering between Kent and Surrey. The work spans the years 1919 to 1947 and its purpose is to show the importance, as well as the hopes, dreams, and aspirations, of the ordinary people who live where two thirds of Britain's population resides, in the suburbs. Taking his cue from Emile Zola and other late nineteenth-century French naturalists, Delderfield stated his intention in a 1964 preface: "I think of this book as a modest attempt to photograph the mood of the suburbs in the period between the break up of the old world and the perambulator days of an entirely new civilisation ushered in by the bleat of Russia's first sputnik in the 'fifties.'"[1]

Volume 1, *The Dreaming Suburb* (1919–40). *The Dreaming Suburb* begins with the end of one war and ends with the beginning of another. Delderfield firmly believed that the people who truly made British policy and who developed political thought were the people of the suburbs whose dreams and aspirations were not only individual manifestations of their personal values and goals but were also the collective unconsciousness of the British people (*A*, vii). The novel is the panoramic of twenty-eight years of British history as background to the lives of five ordinary families living on a suburban street about twelve miles from the heart of London.

The Carver family is headed by Jim Carver, who returns from the trenches early in 1919 only to find that his wife has died of Spanish flu in the great epidemic of that year. His eldest daughter, Louise, has been looking after the other six children. Jim is one of the four pivotal characters in *The Dreaming Suburb*, the others being his son Archie, Esme Fraser, and Elaine Frith.

Jim, the former infantry sergeant, is haunted by his memories of combat, particularly the death of a boy soldier on the last day of fighting, caused by an uncaring and incompetent staff officer. His dream is to see a warless society develop out of the brotherhood of man. He joins the Socialist party and works and fights for socialism. However, the party fails to solve the problems of unemployment and it fails to prevent the rise of fascism, and so Jim eventually runs "the whole gamut of the 'isms' . . . all the way from pacifism to jingoism, with brief stops at every station in between" (*A*, 246). Jim

represents the decent, solid, working-class Englishman, who partici-
pates in class warfare within the limitations that violence must be
avoided and the preservation of the nation must come before all else.

Jim's eldest son, Archie, matured quickly and badly while his
father was away in World War I. He became a black marketeer
during the conflict and then, after marrying Maria Piretta, daughter
of a prosperous Italian grocer, grows wealthy by developing a chain of
"pop-in" stores and by speculating, cheating on taxes, and hoarding.
He has no scruples when it comes to business or women. He cheats
on his wife, for whom he has no love, he schemes to avoid military
service, and he dreams of becoming a millionaire in the new war that
is brewing.

Louise Carver is the hard-working spinsterish surrogate mother-
child who raises the other children for Jim and then belatedly finds a
good mate in a local gardener. Judith, Jim's second daughter, has a
worshipping childhood love for her young neighbor, the romantic
Esme Fraser, and she dreams of marriage and domestic bliss with
Esme, but he is oblivious to her feelings and falls in love with the
beautiful and amoral neighbor, Elaine Frith. Heartbroken, Judith
moves to Devon and eventually marries a young man who is killed at
the very beginning of World War II, just after they were married.

Bernard and Boxer, twin Carvers, are two cut-ups, physical types,
devoted to each other who become motorcycle racers and daredevils,
and who wind up in the British Expeditionary Force in France in
1940. Fetch and Carry, Jim's other set of twins, are infant girls as
the novel begins and they remain background figures in *The Dreaming
Suburb*.

The Fraser family story centers on Esme, whose father, a handsome
young officer, was killed in World War I before he had got to know
his son, and whose mother, the beautiful but not bright Eunice, has
been both encouraging and warding off the marriage suit of Harold
Godbeer, a conservative, good-hearted solicitor's clerk, who loves
Eunice and cares for Esme. When finally Esme is willing to accept
him as a father substitute, the enraptured clerk achieves his dream:
marriage to the lovely, gentle, caring Eunice.

The character of Esme is partly based on Delderfield's own life.
Esme is a child of the suburb who loves to read and dream of
adventures. As a teenager he falls in love with Elaine, who, although
his age, is far more worldly wise, and he loses her partly because he
is too naive to understand and too romantic to meet her physical

needs as a woman. Esme wanders around Britain for years learning to write and carrying a torch for his lost love. He becomes a journalist in London and begins to write for the BBC, and then Elaine comes back in his life just before war breaks out. He, like Delderfield, enlists in the Royal Air Force.

Esme is a romantic dreamer who lives in the past, and his credulous, chivalrous nature handicaps him in his dealing with the pragmatic and amoral Elaine, with whom he finally enters into a doomed marriage. His idealism, naiveté, and virtue make him Delderfield's symbol of the British generation of World War II as Jim Carver symbolizes the generation of World War I.

The Frith family is a troubled and unhappy one. Elaine's mother, Esther, is a sexually cold, unloving, zealously religious woman with an upper-class background, who married a humble antique dealer, Edgar Frith, a shy, little, inexperienced, good-hearted, hen-pecked man, who finally abandons her for a kinder and gentler, sexually more responsive woman, leaving Esther more embittered than ever. Their son, Sydney, is a villainous, cold-hearted sneak who flirts with fascism and when war breaks out quickly gets himself a cozy and safe billet as an Air Force accounts officer.

Elaine is the most fascinating of the Friths and the heroine of the entire saga. She is a sensuous, self-gratifying, and self-serving woman, a literary descendant of Thackeray's heroine of *Vanity Fair*, Becky Sharp. Like Becky, Elaine dreams of a life of luxury and control of men, and she will manipulate men through what she perceives as their pitiful weakness, their libido. She runs away from home after breaking Esme's young heart, works briefly as a hotel clerk, and then becomes the mistress of a broken-down vaudeville magician whom she also assists on stage. Her next affair is with a theatrical agent. Then she joins a circus and becomes involved with the owner, whose wife, the circus strong woman, catches them in bed, gives Elaine a fierce spanking on her bare bottom, and throws her out into the street. At that point Elaine decides she has had enough adventure and decides to opt for security. She skillfully reestablishes her relationship with Esme, who has remained faithful for eight years to the memory of his first love. She inveigles Esme into marriage and they have a child despite Elaine's precautions. However, when war comes and Esme leaves for Air Force service, she becomes the lover of Archie Carver, who plies her with his money, and of a Polish airman, who plies her with his sexuality.

For all her connivence and loose morals Elaine is not an evil person. She may have a selective memory and she may exaggerate from time to time, but she never outright lies, particularly to Esme. She never tells a man she loves him when she does not, and in a sense she gives full sexual value for whatever is the coin to purchase her favor: money, security, or sexual vigor. As Esme dotes madly on her she thinks: "She would give him, she told herself, slightly more than his moneysworth for the time being, but how long she would continue to give it she was not prepared to promise, certainly not till death do them part. If, in the not-too-distant future, he could provide the terrace, and the hammock, and courtiers, the sports car, and the clothes to go with them, then perhaps she might even be willing to continue giving him his moneysworth indefinitely" (A, 405–7).

Clearly, at this stage of his writing career, Delderfield's sexual politics are quite conservative. He would loosen up somewhat in later works. Nevertheless, he is not totally disapproving here of Elaine's decision to meet her own sexual needs and make her way in a man's world by deftly employing Eve's instrument. After all, in her own mind there is always the example of her mother's loveless marriage and the examples of the female drudges around her wearing themselves out and growing old before their time in service to demanding and ungrateful husbands and children. Elaine seems to be one of those characters in a story who takes over from the author and goes her own way despite his original intentions. In this regard his readers share with Delderfield a grudging admiration for his errant heroine.

The Clegg family is an extended one mostly unrelated by blood. Edith and Becky are the spinster daughters of a Devonshire clergyman. Becky lost her mind when, after becoming pregnant, running away with the bounder of a father, and losing her unborn child, she was deserted by her lover. Rescued from the slums of London in a distraught state by Edith, she has never fully recovered from the shock. After their father's death, they moved to the Avenue where Edith must now take in roomers and play piano at a silent movie theater in order to make ends meet. Their first roomer is Ted Hartnell, a stonecutter who turns successful jazz musician and who marries the sharp, pushy singer, Margy. The second is the lovely but speech-impeded Jean McInroy, an illustrator who draws and dreams of meeting and marrying the "perfect English man."

The last family in focus on the Avenue is that of the grocer and widower, Tony Piretta, and his plain daughter, Maria, of whose marriageability he has come to despair. It is he who picks Archie for son-in-law and heir based on Archie's business acumen and his virility, demonstrated by the fact that the young man has impregnated two sisters in the same family almost simultaneously. Above all, Tony dreams of grandchildren and Archie and Maria in their loveless marriage provide him with three to adore.

Of course the ultimate family of *The Dreaming Suburb* and *The Avenue Goes to War* is the Avenue itself. It is the saga's true collective hero. In *The Dreaming Suburb* it experiences and endures the Spanish flu epidemic, the general strike of 1926, the depression, Labor unrest in the 1930s, the Spanish Civil War, the abdication of Edward VIII, and the advent of World War II. Moreover, like the kingdom it ultimately symbolizes, it survives. At the end of *The Dreaming Suburb* Delderfield prepares us for the bombings in the volume to come with these final words: "The houses looked very small, and very still from above, absurdly still for an Avenue at War" (*A*, 446).

Delderfield uses as his narrative technique in both *The Dreaming Suburb* and *The Avenue Goes to War* a five-plot knot in which he interfuses story strands, retarding and withholding culminations, in a successful attempt to renew continually the reader's attention. The realistic narration cuts like a movie from scene to scene, with a human scale foreground series of actions played against a ponderous moving cyclorama of current events. The author continues the technique in the second part of *The Avenue Story*.

Volume 2, *The Avenue Goes to War* (1940–47). *The Dreaming Suburb* began in the light of peace and proceeded to the darkness of war. *The Avenue Goes to War* begins in twilight, moves into the midnight depth of World War II, and emerges into the light of peace. Two thirds of the way through this second long volume Delderfield has Esme state the main theme of the entire opus: "I'd like to propose a toast to the people I've learned to believe in since all this uproar and muddle started. I'd like you to drink to ordinary people in roads like this all over the world" (*A*, 860). The author is celebrating the endurance and the grace of the common person and to Delderfield's great credit he does so without condescension. With this speech the disillusioned Jim Carver realizes: "things are really beginning to work out and give a chap something to hope for in the future!" (*A*, 861).

Although *The Avenue Goes to War* continues the story of all charac-

ters introduced in *The Dreaming Suburb*, it concentrates on four people: Esme, Judith, Archie, and Elaine. Esme takes over the position
of protagonist from Jim Carver, who recedes to somewhat of a Greek
chorus figure. The younger man's marriage to Elaine is disintegrating
while he is in the Royal Air Force. His wife continues to be unfaithful to him with Archie and others. Finally, a tragically bizarre incident occurs by which Esme learns that Elaine has been sleeping with
Archie Carver. Esme's mother, Eunice, has been evacuated to a seemingly safe seaside resort during the Blitz, and she has taken her
granddaughter, Barbara, Elaine's and Esme's child, with her. In one
of those grotesque and senseless incidents in war Eunice is killed by
German strafing planes that just happen to be flying along the coast
at the time she is out strolling a pier with Barbara. The child is
unharmed. Delderfield uses the Luftwaffe as a deus ex flying machina to turn the plot twice more in the novel: when the Avenue is
blitzed and Elaine's mother, Esther, and her brother, Sidney, are
killed; and later, during the raids of the V-1 pilotless missiles, when
the Avenue is smashed even more thoroughly, and Jim loses his
daughter Louise, her husband, and his home, while his friend Harold
Godbeer is seriously wounded.

Meanwhile, when Esme returns unexpectedly to London to tell
Elaine of the tragedy and bring her to Barbara, she is away enjoying
a weekend at Blackpool with Archie. Confronted on her return,
Elaine tries to cover but is caught. Esme takes Barbara to camp
where, coincidentally, his childhood worshipper, Judith, is serving in
the Women's Auxiliary Air Force and getting over the loss of her
soldier husband. Esme and Judith slowly renew their relationship,
fall in love, and plan to marry, which they do only after Esme is
divorced, has become an aerial gunner, is shot down over France, is
rescued by the French Resistance, and is wounded as they fight to get
him out with important papers. Esme also does an intelligence tour
in France evaluating Allied bombing results, a job Delderfield had.
In fact, except for the flying, Esme's military career coincides with
Delderfield's: enlistment, service in the detested Training Command,
intelligence work, and an overseas assignment on the Continent.
Reunited as the war comes to an end, Judith and Esme buy a farm in
Devonshire to spend their lives far from their suburban roots. Their
exodus parallels Delderfield's and even that of the author's wife, May,

who came from a Manchester suburb and who joined him in Devon where for a while they also farmed.

Delderfield sentimentalizes life in the R.A.F. through Esme:

Ever since he had packed up his civilian clothes at the Receiving Depot, Esme had been touched by the kindness and thoughtfulness of the majority of the men around him, touched also by the easy, unselfconscious way in which they shared things. He had acquired the sense of *belonging* that the uniform seemed to give all who wore it. . . . This was something he had been unable to find in civilian life, though he had looked for it at school, at his work, and on his travels about the country. (*A*, 557–58)

Archie, who is as close to a villain as one finds in *The Avenue*, gets his comeuppance in *The Avenue Goes to War*; later he reforms and is given his opportunity for true love and a better life. First, of course, he must suffer. Archie's favorite son, Anthony, has been sent to a fine, expensive school, and to Archie's frustration and chagrin the school has made a leader, a gentleman, a patriot, and an idealist out of him. Tony is the opposite of his father. He shows no interest in business and he spurns Archie's proposals to fiddle his way out of military service. Instead, he joins the Tank Corps and is quickly killed at Tobruk.

Archie's wife, Maria, has grown to hate him and after he gets into trouble with the government for blackmarketeering she steals all his money. Infuriated, Archie drinks too much, goes after Maria, and has an automobile accident in which he kills a girl. He is sent to prison for manslaughter. There he sobers up and straightens out his life. Upon his release Elaine is waiting for him, and they begin a new life together with Archie once more successful in business, but legitimately this time. He has developed an insouciance that will prevent him from repeating the mistakes he made before.

While Archie was in prison, Elaine became engaged to what she thought was the man of her dreams, Lieutenant Woolston Ericssohn of the United States Army. He is a rich Southerner, middle-aged, short, and homely, but he puts her on a pedestal and spends a small fortune on her. Alas, he is lacking in sex drive, and she can not get him into bed in order to consummate the relationship and ensure a marriage proposal. She knows "the thing that makes men tick

. . . *why* people get married, why men take on the endless responsibilities of marriage and even rush gaily into it, with their tongues
hanging out, simply falling over themselves to shoulder the burden
of wife, family, rates, taxes, gas-bills, and God knows what else! It's
all for that, all for having a woman whenever they want one . . ."
(*A*, 791).

Delderfield will not let Elaine's cynical view of marriage stand. He
has her father, Edgar Frith, respond: "There's a good deal more to
marriage than what you say. . . . The comradeship of marriage is
just as important as the physical side, not *more* important, as some
people would argue, but *just* as *important*! It's about fifty-fifty, I'd say,
and the odd thing is that one part seems to be quite useless without
the other" (*A*, 791).

Although Elaine finally does trick the bloodless Ericssohn into
proposing marriage, she throws him over at the last moment because
she cannot stand his racial bigotry, his deification of her, and his lack
of sexuality. Wisely, she chooses her true equal, Archie.

The stories of the other characters from *The Dreaming Suburb* are
concluded in *The Avenue Goes to War*. Jim's twin sons, Bernard and
Boxer, as commandos, fight in the disastrous raid at Dieppe, are
reported missing, and presumed dead. Jim grieves for them, but
they have not been killed. Bernard has been badly wounded and now
for the first time Boxer takes care of him. Boxer gives up his chance
of escaping off the beach and instead he gets medical treatment for
Bernard. Both are taken prisoner. Bernard has an arm amputated and
is repatriated to Britain where he is reunited with Edgar Frith's
stepdaughter, Pippa, with whom he has fallen in love. Despite his
grievous wound, he is able to make a useful life for himself thanks to
his wife Pippa and their families.

Boxer learns to think and act independently as a prisoner of war.
In the final days of the conflict he escapes and becomes the head of a
band of refugees, ex-slave workers, and defeated German soldiers
anxious to surrender to the Americans or British. Boxer, previously
always the follower, is now a leader, and he brings his charges to
safety, eventually falling in love with one of them, the Russian girl
Olga, whom he marries after the war.

Fetch and Carry, Jim's twin daughters, fall in love with American
G.I.s and after the war they go to the United States as war brides.

Ted and Margery Hartnell are separated during the war. He serves
heroically in the merchant marine and is the first resident of the

Avenue to receive a medal. Margy serves as an entertainer overseas. Ted survives torpedoing and strafing. Finally, they are reunited and take up their entertainment careers at a seaside resort so Ted can remain near the element he has grown to love. Jean McInroy finally wins her perfect English man by rescuing Chief Officer Hargreaves from beneath a dangerous pile of bomb rubble. His hearing has been destroyed in the blast so that now her speech impediment does not matter.

Harold Godbeer, Esme's stepfather, and Jim Carver become best of pals as they wait out the war together. Their friendship symbolizes the coming together of the middle class and the working class in the joint patriotic effort during World War II. When Harold wants to give up on life after his wife's death and his own debilitating wounds, Jim gives him the courage to endure and persevere.

Edith Cleggs and Jim mutually support each other during the conflict. A fondness grows between them, and after Edith's sister Becky is killed in the V-1 blast and both hers and Jim's home have been destroyed, Jim proposes marriage and is accepted. The sixty-year-olds find happiness too. The reformed Archie, grateful to both of them for aiding him in his dark hours, buys them one of the few surviving houses on the Avenue as a wedding present.

Although it is to be assumed that all the characters, having suffered, endured, and survived, will live happily ever after, the Avenue itself, almost destroyed by bombs, emerges from the war forever maimed. The street is cut and reshaped, and renamed Manor Road. Its humbler name and smaller dimensions symbolize the shrinking of the British Empire. It is less grand but homier and more friendly.

The Avenue Story was an auspicious start to Delderfield's career as a writer of sagas. It contains a balanced mix of history, melodramatic incident, and vital characterization. If it is self-congratulatory as a piece of British literature, it nevertheless portrays all of its denizens on a human scale. After all, if *The Avenue Story* glorifies a type of person, it glorifies the survivor, not the hero; the endurer, not the aggressor. Salt may be common, but it is important and it is necessary. When Delderfield lifts the rooftops of the homes on Manor Park Avenue he finds the salt of the earth, common and yet not so common folk who dream and whose dreams are important to a great nation.

Delderfield's style in *The Avenue Story* is brisk, easy to read, yet profound. One is reminded of the economical style of Nevil Shute in

such historical novels as *A Town Called Alice* (1949), his story of
Anglo-Australian ordeals in Southeast Asia during World War II.
Both authors are consumately skilled in integrating history and
fiction. Both use direct, purposeful discourse to punch hard and
straight.

Diana

Diana is a 666-page, two-volume love story. Set in the lovely West
Country of England, it chronicles the relationship between John
Leigh, a cockney orphan living with relatives in Devonshire, and
Diana Gayelorde-Sutton, the beautiful, wild, headstrong daughter of
the local squirearchy. Narrated in the first person by John, the tale
encompasses eighteen years, 1930 through 1948, from the time John
is fifteen and Diana fourteen, to Diana's death about three years after
World War II comes to an end. This novel is based on, and makes
frequent reference to, the classic Victorian historical romance, *Lorna
Doone* (1869), by R. D. Blackmore, who subtitled his novel *A
Romance of Exmore*. In *Lorna Doone* a local farmer's son, John (Jan)
Ridd, fights for and eventually wins the love of the beautiful, high-
born Lorna Doone, daughter of the leader of an outlaw clan who
reputedly killed John's father. Delderfield's Diana continually calls
John "Jan Ridd." *Diana* and *Lorna Doone* both celebrate the triumph
of love over differing family backgrounds and the animosity of parents, through the sacrifice, patience, commitment, and endurance of
the lovers.

There Was a Fair Maid Dwelling. R. F. Delderfield's second
saga is, like *The Avenue*, almost as much a story of a place, as it is of
people. The place introduced in *There Was a Fair Maid Dwelling* is
called Sennacharib [*sic*] by the young lovers, Diana and John, who
first meet in a mystical and beautiful Devon woods, where the leaves
seem to whisper "Assyria—Assyria—Assyria."[2] Thus they name their
tiny, magical valley kingdom of woods, hills, pastures, streams, and
seacoast after Lord Byron's poem, "The Destruction of Sennacherib,"
the first line of which is "The Assyrian came down like the wolf on
the fold."

John Leigh, the narrator, whose Bildungsroman *Diana* is, first
comes to know about Sennacharib "the country, the woods, dove-grey
and russet, the white ribbon of road, the smoky, purple woods
beyond, the patchwork green of the pasture, the red brown of the

plowed land . . ." (*D*, 4) through the memory of his mother, Devon-born but married to a Londoner and living her life in the capital. At the novel's opening, John, now an orphan, has just come from London to live in Devon with his Uncle Luke, a used furniture dealer, and his Aunt Thizra. When the city-bred boy sees the countryside for the first time, "The sensation was as much physical as spiritual. It was as though something had struck me a sudden blow in the pit of the stomach, a fierce winding blow that made me reel and reach out to steady myself against the smooth bole of the nearest beech" (*D*, 3). It was love at first sight for the locale as well as for the girl Diana, the daughter of the manor who rescues him from the gamekeeper who has caught John trespassing in the woods owned by her industrialist father, Eric Gayelorde-Sutton. John is fifteen, Diana less than a year younger. A later reference to date gives the year as 1927 (*D*, 61), but since Diana is twenty-one on 18 June 1937 (*D*, 260), the year must be 1930. Delderfield is a bit careless with dates in the beginning.

The bond between the lovers is always more spiritual than physical. It is based on their shared love of the countryside. Diana states it succinctly: "I think that's what I like about you . . . you feel about this place as if it were something alive, like an animal. That's exactly how I feel but I don't think I'd have known that if I hadn't met you that day in the woods" (*D*, 65).

The relationship between the adolescents remains an adventure, particularly for Diana, who uses it as a way to get back at her domineering and snobbish mother, who, of course, would never allow her daughter, whom she calls Emerald, to befriend a cockney-born lower-middle-class lad. For John the relationship is his rite of passage both into the adult world and into the world of achievement. Warned that the beautiful, vivacious, well-educated, sophisticated girl is beyond his expectations, John determines to win her for his eventual wife and in so doing sets about to improve his lot and station in life. John Ridd will be his model. Symbolically, he gives Diana a copy of *Lorna Doone* for her fifteenth birthday. He learns to ride expertly, he becomes fluent in French, he leaves his job in Uncle Luke's shop to work for his Uncle Reuben, the editor of the *Whinmouth and District Observer*, he works temporarily as a journalist in London, writes a history, and returns as the editor of the weekly newspaper when Uncle Reuben takes ill and then dies.

The love affair has multiple ups and downs, and John struggles to hold on to Diana. They meet surreptitiously. They run away to an offshore island for a brief idyll as an innocent Adam and Eve, and upon their return Diana is subjected by her mother to a humiliating examination in order to prove her virginity and prevent prosecution of John. On her eighteenth birthday Diana sneaks John into the family mansion, Heronslea, during the party, and when all the guests have left she gives herself to him in her own bed. Her motivation is partly out of love for her ever faithful suitor, partly as a parting gift to the young man who memorializes her adolescence now passed, and partly as the ultimate revenge on her overly possessive, overly protective mother.

To John's great shock, shortly after their tryst, which to him sealed their love, Diana sends him a Dear John letter from New York ending their relationship because she feels that their differing up-bringings and expectations would prevent happiness in marriage. All they would have was sex.

Uncle Reuben, an old bachelor, and in his sickbed, nevertheless steels the disheartened young man: "If you want this girl as much as you say you do, then in God's name go in and get her! . . . If she's written you this mealymouthed letter because she thinks you've always accepted the situation and are therefore likely to go on doing so, then show her different. Thumb your nose at her background, tan her backside if you have to, and she'll want you the more for it!" (*D*, 270). Unfortunately, there is a lot of macho man advice in Delderfield's fiction. He admittedly was addicted to the films of his youth and maturity, and it appears that the Hollywood concept of the he-man hero conquering heroines with a rough sex approach appealed to the author. John never spanks Diana, but he does strike her with a riding switch much later on when she is trying to control their destiny, and the physical assault excites her sexually and they make furious love (*D*, 331–33).

Meanwhile, however, John plays it cool and bides his time. Inevitably, Diana is caught up in the aristocratic fast set. She begins drinking too much and is involved in an automobile accident, a head-on collision in which a young man and his pregnant wife are killed. Spiritually, emotionally, and physically exhausted she calls on John to save her, and he takes her back to Devon and Sennacharib where she is renewed. Now Diana's industrialist father has no objec-tion to a marriage between his daughter and John. Rather, he en-courages it because his financial affairs are in great disorder and he sees that John is the man who can protect that which is best in his daughter: Diana the goddess of the forest of Sennacharib, from Emerald, the society bauble. But it is too late. Mr. Gayelorde-Sutton goes bankrupt quickly, commits suicide, and Diana panics. She leaves John on a pretext and quickly marries an effete but fabulously wealthy young Frenchman, Yves de Royden, and goes to live in France.

John is nearly destroyed by this betrayal and becomes a recluse and misanthrope. Slowly, however, Sennacharib restores him too, and he comes to appreciate all that Diana has given to him and how she has enriched his life. The peripeteia occurs when in his despair he hunts the small animals of the woods as if to wreak a revenge on them, and he sees once more a pair of buzzards, a sight that almost always has preceded meeting of the lovers (*D*, 358). He tries to destroy them but fails and in doing so he begins his resurrection.

There is a long caesura in *There Was a Fair Maid Dwelling*. The story resumes in May 1940. John is in the army, an officer with the British Expeditionary Force retreating from France after the successful German blitzkrieg. He is evacuating civilians from Bordeaux when he receives a note from Diana asking him to come and get her. She is trying to rescue five children, one of whom is hers, and, as John learns to his great surprise, his. She was pregnant when she deserted him.

Diana will not return to England with John and her charges but stays in France to join the Resistance, not so much out of patriotism but primarily because it is another chance at adventure. Furthermore, the de Roydens have joined the Nazis and this angers her. John takes the children, including their Yvonne, to Devon where they live in Heronslea, which Diana has turned into an orphanage for young war victims. As John wonders about Diana's fate and the outcome of the war, he is comforted because "Children were laughing in Senacharib" (*D*, 380).

The reader realizes that there is more to come. John's determination to win Diana for himself demands a more decisive outcome and thus the sequel, *The Unjust Skies*, is prepared for. However, although the plot craving in the reader has not been satiated, the richly developed characterizations and the mercurial changes, the refreshing simplicity, awkwardness, and excitements of young love, provide quite a banquet for readers of *There Was a Fair Maid Dwelling*.

The Unjust Skies. *There Was a Fair Maid Dwelling* is a romance of childhood and youth. Its sequel, *The Unjust Skies*, is for three fourths of its contents a World War II espionage adventure. The title comes from William Butler Yeats's poem "Cold Heaven" in which the newly released spirit or ghost of a dead person "is sent / Out naked on the roads" where it is "stricken / By the injustice of the skies for punishment." The implication for the second part of the Diana story is that the pain and suffering the hero and heroine endure is a punishment for their youthful folly, but for Diana, like King Lear, she is "more sinned against than sinning."

The Unjust Skies picks up John Leigh's narrative *in media res*. It is 1942. He is a member of Special Operations, a British secret agent in German-occupied Paris, a few miles away from the suburban mansion in which Diana is residing with her husband, Yves de Royden, whom it turns out is a Nazi collaborator and homosexual. Diana and John have become lovers again and they have been involved in a plot to kill Diana's previous lover, Pierce Rance, a sadistic French scientist working on a secret weapon for the Germans, and to kidnap Yves and bring him and the plans for a component of the weapons being made in his factory to England. It is an exciting and intriguing start to a sequel to a fairly placid romance. The sex in *There Was a Fair Maid Dwelling* is limited almost exclusively to idyllic trysts between two young lovers. In *The Unjust Skies* the reader quickly learns that Diana has been, as she succinctly states, "whoring without a fee" (*D*, 440). Furthermore, John has already seen her undergoing sadomasochistic sexual humiliation at the hands of Rance, whom he has now killed. As John waits for the strike against Yves the novel proceeds to a five-chapter, ninety-five page flashback.

John, upon returning from France with his daughter and the other children rescued by Diana, has met and quickly married Allison, whom he never truly loved. Unfortunately, she is killed by German fighter planes in a hit and run attack similar to the one that killed Eunice Fraser in *The Avenue Story*. Hoping for action, John transfers to the Royal Air Force but because of poor vision, a medical problem he shares with his author, is denied combat air-crew status. He is then asked to serve as a secret agent by Captain Raoul de Royden, a cousin of Yves and a gallant Free French officer who has been sent to England by Diana to enlist John's aid in the French Underground's plan to thwart the production of a German secret weapon, what presumably would become the V-1 missile, being built in part in Yves's factory.

Diana has sent him a letter through Raoul in which she gives the first hint that Delderfield has enlarged the theme of the saga. In *There Was a Fair Maid Dwelling* Sennacharib symbolized the idyllic world of childhood and youth as well as the pastoral countryside where nature remains unspoiled. In *The Unjust Skies* Sennacharib comes to stand for all of Britain, city and country, and most significantly its humanistic and democratic values. Diana says in her letter: "I don't deserve (your) loyalty but Sennacharib does and, after all, that's what this war is about, isn't it, Jan?" (*D*, 398).

However, John also senses that the war is yet another game for the playgirl Diana and he refuses to help her at first. His wife is still unburied and he goes off to arrange the funeral at which Diana suddenly appears, having talked the French and British secret services into flying her to England to convince John to help her. His fluency in French, his artillery training, and his knowledge of the antique trade could both offer him a cover as a French-Canadian art expert and give the Underground some technical expertise in ballistics. John finally agrees, not out of patriotism but for Diana, to whom he still feels a deep bond.

After a brief but intense period of espionage training, John is reunited with Diana in France where they become lovers again. Just before going into action Diana confesses her past promiscuities, the details of her affair with Rance, and the fact that she was pregnant with Rance's child when she went to England to see John. The reader learns later that Diana had an abortion because she could not participate in the murder of a man whose child was in her womb.

As anticipated, Rance calls upon his lover, requiring once more her drugged sexual slavery to which Diana submits with both disgust and lust. John shoots Rance in the midst of his reverie. They take the collaborator's keys and papers. John, who resembles Rance, the reason that Diana fell in love with the sadist, will pose as the dead scientist and gain access to Yves's mansion where he and Diana will kidnap her husband.

The long flashback, the most exciting part of *The Unjust Skies*, is over, and John and Diana go into action again, kidnapping Yves, but they botch the job. John is struck down by Yves and Diana must kill her husband by running him over with his own Mercedes. Awakening in an English hospital, John learns that both Diana and he have been rescued and the papers they brought back are useful to the Allied cause. Recovering, John takes charge of Diana and the relationship in the usual Delderfield manner, as Diana finally admits: "From now on I'll always go along with you. You're the boss, Jan! Don't forget that, don't ever forget it, for your own sake and mine. Not even if you have to wallop me into remembering every so often!" (*D*, 522).

It appears that the love story of John and Diana is coming to an end as they settle with Yvonne in Heronslea and are married at last, but this is not to be, for, almost anticlimactically, John again is asked to volunteer for Special Operations in France. He does so despite the fact that Diana has a weak heart and that she is trying to become pregnant to give him a son. His motivation now is patriotism: "How much did I owe the Allied cause? . . . If the Allies had not stood up to the Nazis in 1940, Sennacharib would have ceased to exist, for me or anyone else, of that I was certain. For me Sennarcharib *was* the nation" (*D*, 564).

Before returning to Occupied France, this time to lead a team of saboteurs ordered to take out a section of strategic rail to coincide with D Day, John comes to realize that Diana is a pagan, that her spirit and her body are consecrated to nature, a part of and the essence of Sennacharib. Going to the beach early one morning John sees Diana standing nude at the water's edge with wavelets breaking at her feet. She is rigid and preoccupied. Her arms are extended seaward in supplication. Unknown to her husband, she is praying to nature for a man child to meet "the primeval need of every woman, to bear male children for the man who is the focal point of her existence" (*D*, 555). John observes to himself that his beautiful wife "was engaged in a form of supplication that had nothing whatever to do with Christianity, or with any known cult, but with something that had its roots in far-off centuries when tribes acknowledged allegiance to the things about them, the moon, stars, and wind, to the red sun now rising from behind the headland and laying its rays across the bay" (*D*, 545).

In France John is convinced that he will never see Diana again. However, she manages to get over in order to make sure he has a chance to survive. There is an exciting battle scene, reminiscent of *The Avenue Story*. His mission is successful, but he is wounded when they are escaping, and Diana, in order to give her husband a slim chance to survive, allows herself to be captured by the Germans. John recovers with the Partisans at whose side he fights ferociously for months until he learns that Diana is alive and being held as a hostage. In a rescue attempt she is badly wounded and paralyzed. In England she undergoes a series of operations but to no avail. The war ends. Slowly the life seeps from her body as if her spirit wishes to leave Heronslea and return to the woods and waters of Sennacharib. As John nurses her she turns to the reading and then the writing of poetry. Near death after three years of stoic suffering she has John carry her on horseback to their favorite hill in Sennacharib. As she requested before death, she is cremated and, in one of the two fine and moving poems Delderfield gives Diana, evidence by the way of some considerable poetic skill on his behalf, she instructs him: "On Foxhayes edge go scatter my ashes" (*D*, 665).

Unable to go on, John is saved by a posthumous letter from Diana urging him to enjoy his life. The symbolic buzzards appear again over Teasel Wood. The grieving John is not surprised. "Diana had always promised that they would come wheeling in the moment we were reunited" (*D*, 666).

The touching ending is full of the refulgence and redolence of the Devon woods. The reader is deeply moved by the sense of both finality and beginning that Delderfield evokes. His storytelling ability, his inexhaustible supply of convincing description, and his supply of characters about whom the reader must really care, overcome any incredulity and weariness.

Both *The Avenue Story* and *Diana* are prose monuments to the British spirit: city, suburb, and country that brought a beleagured but undaunted people through a terrible half century. That is what Delderfield celebrates in his first two sagas and this is what won him the vast following in the English-speaking world, a following he kept through the even greater successes of his later sagas.

Chapter Five
Other Tacks

During the 1960s, while working at a breakneck pace on his sagas, R. F. Delderfield, seemingly as a kind of "Literary Therapy,"[1] experimented with five shorter novels each one quite different from the next. The first is a comic novel, *Stop at a Winner* (1961). The next is a satire on middle-aged love and marriage, *The Spring Madness of Mr. Sermon* (1963). The third, *Too Few for Drums* (1964), is Delderfield's last historical romance. *Cheap Day Return* (1967) is a bitter reminiscence of youth. Finally, *Come Home Charlie and Face Them* (1969) is a crime story. None of these novels are major fictional efforts. They often contain snipets of plot, subject, and characterization used earlier by Delderfield in play or novel, and they draw heavily on his experience in World War II, his early career in provincial journalism, and his knowledge of and appreciation for small-town English life. Yet each of these novels is readable, and each contains some factor of Delderfield's fictional skill, either his traditionally good, strong plot, or a character or two not easily forgotten.

Stop at a Winner

World War II, unlike other modern wars, spawned a great number of satires even while the war was in progress. The massive military establishments of all the combatant nations were ripe for debunking. Delderfield, who spent much of military service as an enlisted clerk in the Royal Air Force shuffling papers in backwater camps, had to take another crack at the military, this time in the novel, but much in the same way he had treated military life in two plays: *Worm's Eye View* and *Waggonload o' Monkeys: Further Adventures of Porter and Taffy*. In fact, Porter is resurrected as one of the two protagonists of *Stop at a Winner*, now satirically named Horace Pope but still the same shifty cockney, ever on the make, running profitable "fiddles," exploiting the confused R.A.F. bureaucracy, and avoiding matrimony. *Stop at a Winner* is related to, but not nearly as profound as, the masterpiece of military black humor farce, Joseph Heller's *Catch 22* (1961), and like Delderfield's R.A.F. plays, it reminds the reader of Mac Hyman's service satire *No Time for Sergeants* (1954).

Horace Pope has attempted to avoid conscription and failed. Although removed from his London market stall he remains the entrepreneur in business for himself at the expense of everyone and everything else, especially the R.A.F., whose wood, fuel, and services he gladly sells for personal gain. His one other loyalty besides that to himself is to his odd-match buddy, Pedlar Pasco, six feet four inches and strong as an ox but with a mind only slightly more advanced than Lenny's in John Steinbeck's *Of Mice and Men* (1937), a character to whom he bears a strong but nontragic resemblance. Pedlar, a Gypsy, has joined the R.A.F. to avoid going home to his fierce mother on Exmoor whose money he has misspent on beer. Pope and Pedlar make a perfect team: brains and brawn. They are a sight:

Pedlar topped Pope by at least fourteen inches and although Pope was sturdy and well-knit he looked like a starvling alongside his huge, lumbering friend. Pedlar's strawlike hair, shorn to a stubble under the Air Force barber's clippers, stuck out at a variety of angles from beneath the sweatband of his lightly perched glengarry, but Pope had paid the barber an extra half-crown for a civilian haircut, and his black widow's peak, gleaming with vasoline, curved down to meet his arched, Mephistophelian brows, emphasizing the neat, dapper appearance created by his well-fitting uniform (the result of a substantial tip in the tailor's shop) and his twinkling officer's shoes, authorized by a forged chit describing a mythical bunion, now under treatment.[2]

The picaresque antiheroes proceed to make war not on the Germans but on the nearer enemies: authorities, grasping civilians, officers, non-coms, and parents of attractive girls. The incidents that these peripatetic hustlers provoke are funny indeed, ranging from driving a martinet of a drill instructor mad and selling cushy postings to men already assigned to the desired locales but unaware that their orders were in progress, to peddling R.A.F. meat and gas to greedy civilian blackmarketeers who invariably get caught and lose either their health by working a gas siphon the wrong way, or their daughter's chastity by trusting the elusive Pope, a man determined to remain free of all controls, especially martial and marital ones.

In order to help Pope flee from the butcher father of a girl his friend has impregnated, Pedlar, who is not supposed to think, foolishly volunteers them for overseas duty in the war zone. Pope is distraught, but fortunately they are caught in an air raid at the port of embarkation while Pedlar is engaged in a beer-drinking contest for the honor of England against Australia, and though unhurt they manage to convince the medical types that they are casualties, and they are sent upon "recovery" to an idyllic camp with an "Arcadian air . . . (where) it would not have seemed very surprising if, on taking a stroll down the main avenue between the sagging, weed screened-huts, one could have heard the toot of the merry, merry pipes of Pan, or seen an airman attired as a shepherd chasing a blue-uniformed nymph across the box-strewn parade ground" (SW, 132).

Here Pope and Pedlar work a fiddle that gets valuable wood crates into the hands of Pope's London friends. However, after they try cooking for the camp and their tapioca pudding provokes a riot, they are transferred from that military paradise to Devon and an American airbase where they are outfiddled by the Yanks in an attempt to turn a run down pub into a moneymaker by importing sexy barmaids from London and inventing a ghost. The incident is right out of Delderfield's play, *Waggonload o' Monkeys*.

As the war progresses the dynamic duo find themselves in France driving supply trucks, only to wind up accidentally in the middle of the Battle of the Bulge in which they become heroes to the Americans by holding up the German advance. Delderfield gets another chance to write a good battle scene, but Pope and Pedlar are unconvincing in their combat roles.

With the end of the war and discharge Pope decides that America is the place for them to work their fiddles in the future. It seems possible that Delderfield may have considered a sequel depicting the adventures of these two British originals in the homeland of their Yank allies with whom they had shared several adventures. These not too innocents abroad would have provided opportunities for Delderfield to continue his bemused observations of Americans and their culture begun in *The Avenue Story*.

The great strength of *Stop at a Winner* is the convincing and delightful characterizations of Pedlar and Pope. These fictional originals have a charm and warmth that overcome the gross improbability, even for farce, of some stops on their odyssey and the episodal structure of the novel. They do little harm, of course, and they often stand for the revenge of the enlisted man on incompetent officers, disdainful civilians, and a world that insists on incorporating unwilling little people into great events. *Stop at a Winner* is a book that Delderfield, the ex-airman, had to get off his chest and one he thoroughly enjoyed writing.

The Spring Madness of Mr. Sermon

The year is 1961 and Sebastian Sermon, a schoolmaster at a second-rate school, married to a disdainful but wealthy and attractive wife and seemingly content with his life, suddenly undergoes, as his fiftieth year approaches, what his fatuous headmaster, Reverend Hawley, calls "Change of life, dear fellow! Physiologically, the change is supposed to be the prerogative of women but I've never believed this, not entirely. Men undergo a change in the late forties and sometimes the manifestation is more subtle than that of its feminine counterpart."[3] Sebastian's change, however, manifests itself in his banging the head of a goading, loutish schoolboy against a water pipe, quitting his job, going home to his indifferent wife and spanking her, and then walking out on his family to undertake a walking tour of the West Country coast in order to find both his Avalon and his true self. He does find both in a seaside resort town after a series of adventures.

Once more Delderfield creates a protagonist who is exactly his own age. The writer and the book's hero have other things in common. Sebastian deserts his home in a London suburb to find happiness in Devon. He has served in World War II as an enlisted man because his eyesight prevented him from being commissioned, an experience shared by Delderfield for much of his military career. Eventually,

Sebastian resumes his teaching career with his chastised wife by his side at a fine Devon public school reminiscent of Delderfield's West Buckfield.

Sebastian's adventures include learning to wheel and deal in the antique trade, becoming a minor official in the seaside town, having an affair with his attractive landlady, Olga, and rescuing an injured bus driver. But most significantly he meets and eventually is seduced by a beautiful and much younger woman, Rachel Grey, at whose side he rescues the trapped animals of the local zoo who are endangered by a storm and a flood. In her arms he learns to make love forcefully. Rachel thinks: "He's never really had a woman before, not really, not like this! Those other women, his wife and that experimental spinster of his, they only took from him. . . . They didn't yield anything of themselves in the process because he was too gentle and considerate and had so much essential kindness. Now perhaps he's learned something about women, that it doesn't do always to be kind and gentle and after—you—madam!" (*SM*, 724–75).

Sebastian's encounter with Rachel restores his sense of manhood and gives him self-confidence as a lover so that he is able to win his wife over to the idea of not only returning to his bed but also giving up her social life in the suburbs and moving with him to the Devon school in which he recommences teaching. At fifty, as the novel ends, he becomes an expectant father.

Like Shakespeare's *Taming of the Shrew*, *The Spring Madness of Mr. Sermon* is the dream of a middle-aged male chauvinist. Although many of the episodes are both amusing and gratifying, the overall theme that it takes caveman tactics in life and love for men to succeed and to make woman truly happy and satisfied was absurdly out of date even at the time of writing, and, of course, is in retrospect both ethically and morally incorrect. As Delderfield is hard on the military in *Stop at a Winner*, he is almost as hard on women here. His females are all stereotypes: wife Sybil is a too busy social butterfly inappreciative of her husband's qualities; landlady Olga is quickly brought out of her lonely cocoon by sex; nymph Rachel is wise in the ways of youth and easy sex. Of course, they are all sexually attractive, and they know or come to learn that a woman's fulfillment in life can only come through her role as lover to a strong man.

Seen as a story about middle-aged male needs to be assured of sexual potency, *The Spring Madness of Mr. Sermon* seems less amusing.

Its view of male-female relations is peacock proud on one side and impoverished on the other. However, if the reader can move beyond the sexual absurdities, he or she can revel somewhat in the liberation of a Caspar Milquetoast.

Too Few for Drums

Too Few for Drums was falsely promoted as a book for adolescents. In fact, it is quite different in tone from Delderfield's one true book for youth, *The Adventures of Ben Gunn* (1956), in that it contains much realistic violence and an overt sexual theme. The time is the Napoleonic period and a British army is retreating in Portugal. Nineteen-year-old Ensign Keith Graham is left in charge of a file of eight soldiers when his captain is killed by a French sharpshooter and his small unit is cut off from the main body of British troops because a bridge is blown too soon. The inexperienced Graham must somehow lead his men to safety.

Like *Seven Man from Gascony*, *Too Few for Drums* is the story of a small unit of men in war. This time the troopers are British, there is only one campaign, and the protagonist is an officer. However, as in *Seven Men of Gascony*, there is an experienced battle-wise sergeant to help him with command. Sergeant Fox is not as colorful as Sergeant Jean Ticquet nor does he last as long, for this is callow and green Ensign Graham's Bildungsroman. Early in the retreat Fox sacrifices himself in a rear guard action to allow the file to continue to survive French attacks. The other men in the file are of less use to Graham: Lickspittle and Croyde are ex-cons and looters, Morgan is a Bible-thumping Welsh Methodist, Strawbridge is a giant countryman but not bright, and Watson is an ex-chimney sweep; but Lockhart, the former game keeper, is a steady soldier, and there is a plucky little drummer boy name Curle with them too. Along the desperate flight from the Mondego to the banks of the Tagus they come across the beautiful camp follower, Gwyneth, a Welsh girl of twenty-three, but wise and experienced far beyond her years. She is a stoic soldier's woman who has had many "husbands," the latest of whom has just died when the band discovers and takes her with them.

Gwyneth is the least believable character in *Too Few for Drums*. She knows as much about British strategy as the Duke of Wellington and her field wisdom is that of a veteran combat infantryman. Nicholette, the camp follower in *Seven Men of Gascony*, is a far more realistic portrayal of a woman with the army, at least as far as her role in combat and decision-making is concerned. Delderfield uses Gwyneth to propose his view that boys become men after sex, for when she initiates Graham into the rites of Venus the boy soldier is instantly transformed into a competent and respected leader. In fact, Graham's maturation is the result of her solicitude and the pressures of the responsibility for his men that the fortunes of war have thrust upon his untried shoulders.

Delderfield, unlikely though it seems, also uses Gwyneth to mouth his own Francophile views in regard to the Napoleonic system of government early in the nineteenth century as opposed to the more repressive system in England. Delderfield decries the British military organization in which officer's rank is either inherited or bought, while he praises the more democratic Napoleonic system, which elevates men according to merit. The British persevere and win only because of their bravery, resourcefulness, and pluck: in essence, despite the system, not because of it.

For thirty days the lost band battles starvation, French cavalry, treacherous Portugese "allies," and two fast-running rivers they must cross. One by one the redcoats are picked off. Morgan is speared by a lancer. Lickspittle tries to rape Gwyneth and she blows his head off, exclaiming: "I lay for soldiers, not for the dregs of the jails, Mr. Graham!"[4] Strawbridge is hacked to death trying to retrieve his beloved musket, his "Brown Bess," from Portugese thieves. Croyde drowns when he refuses to leave behind his money belt filled with looted silver coins.

Their prodigious effort seems doomed when they are suddenly captured. However, the wounded Lockhart steals a file, allowing Graham, Watson, Curle, and Gwyneth to escape. Exhausted, and at the end of their tether, the ragged remnant is rescued by a British gunboat and Graham is promoted to lieutenant for his intrepidness and for the valuable intelligence he has brought back from the field. Curle is ill with tuberculosis but will be discharged and sent to recover with Graham's wealthy family in England. Watson becomes Graham's servant, and Gwyneth, who once made "you a man fit to lead" (*TFD*, 111), will find another "husband," but will always be ready to "help" her young officer prepare for battle in the future. Furthermore, she has a secret she will never share with her lover: she has his child in her womb, surely a son who will be a valorous soldier like his father and a wily survivor like his mother. In short: the ideal warrior.

Although credulity is somewhat strained, *Too Few for Drums* reads as fast, as sticky, and as bloody as any C. S. Forester tale of the struggle with Napoleon. In fact, in both locale and characterization the novel is reminiscent of two tales of the Penninsular campaign by Forester: *Death to the French* (1932) and *The Gun* (1933). Forester and Delderfield shared the historian's interest in the Napoleonic period, each writing both novels and historical studies of that era.

Too Few for Drums lacks the scope and verisimilitude of *Seven Men of Gascony*. The later novel leaves the reader with the feeling that he or she knows what it is to be caught up in endless, wasteful, all-destroying war, whereas *Too Few for Drums* is almost as much an unorthodox manual of how to make a good junior officer as it is a saga of a campaign. Nevertheless, Delderfield's unfailing narrative ability, his palette of electric colors, and his fine eye for military detail make *Too Few for Drums* another tale the reader finishes with great reluctance.

Cheap Day Return

Cheap Day Return is a strange first person novel about the regrets of a middle-aged man who, although successful in the outside world of great events and important people, finds his life unfulfilled and without meaning because he betrayed an innocent love and deserted his small town as a youth. As a result he has found neither happiness nor satisfaction in life or work.

The hero is Kent Stuart, nicknamed Pip because like the hero of *Great Expectations* he was an orphaned child when he was brought to the small, sleepy seaside resort town of Redcliffe Bay. The novel consists almost entirely of a flashback as the fifty year old returns to town thirty years after he departed. It is "curiosity and the strong tug of nostalgia" that motivates Pip's return.[5] And it is nostalgia for the simpler life and simpler ways of the seaside town of Exmouth in the 1930s that motivates Delderfield's hand. The year is 1962, Pip is Delderfield's age, the events recalled occur in 1932.

Pip is a photographer's apprentice about to inherit the business from his dissolute boss. He casually courts Esta Wallace, the intelligent, pretty, but provincial daughter of an ironmonger, who is in

training to become a nurse. Esta has an acute sense of place; she
understands the hold an environment can have on a person, a hold
Pip chaffs at: " 'Oh, it's not just a question of locale!' she said. . . .
'I think that's where people like us can't see the wood from the trees.
It's much more a matter of—well—belonging' " (CDR, 106).

However, Pip eschews the very thought of settling down to a
lifetime of baby carriage, bills, and beer in the neighborhood pub.
Enter the older woman, Lorna Morney-Sutcliffe, the thirty-one-year-
old, Paris-born wife of the local doctor. A slightly superannuated
flapper type, she is an English Madame Bovary without the latter's
basic innocence and depth of passion. She meets Pip at a benefit
dance and makes him feel discontent with his future in Redcliffe Bay,
and then seduces him with French kisses, nude swimming, and his
first taste of sex.

Frenzied with love and sexual desire, Pip abandons apple-cheeked
Esta and plans to run away with his seductress. Lorna, however, has
only been using him, enjoying his adulation and his body. She
implies that her husband is an indifferent fool who does not care
about her, and Pip comes to despise the busy and ambitious physician. At the last moment, however, Lorna decides to run away with a
different young man, Mike Shapely, a store manager known locally as
the "Sixpenny Sheik." They flee in the doctor's yacht, a storm arises,
and they both die. Meanwhile, Pip has been seriously injured in a
cliff fall following his last assignation with Lorna, who has told Pip
that her husband is coming when in fact she was expecting her other
lover. Lorna Morney-Sutcliffe is no Lorna Doone.

Dr. Morney-Sutcliffe slowly emerges as a decent, sensitive human
being, compassionate and understanding about his wife's "nympho-
mania," which he considers mental illness. He also turns out to be a
superb physician who saves Pip's arm from almost certain amputation
and helps to heal Pip's injured soul. Matured in the fire of his
youthful passion and chastised by the realization of his own folly, Pip
leaves Redcliffe Bay. Upon returning thirty years later, after a successful career as an internationally renown photographer, he is dis-
mayed by the changes made in the name of progress and
commercialism and by "the telly and the transistor, the small car and
the tourist agencies" (CDR, 10). However, as the story ends, Pip
learns that Esta, who married Pip's seemingly slow-witted rival,
Cecil Trumper, did quite well for herself after all. Cecil turned out to
be a successful land developer who made a fortune, was knighted,

and conveniently died a short time before Pip's reappearance. Pip telephones Esta, who is glad to hear from him, and the reader is left with the distinct impression of a forthcoming happy ending to Pip's long exile from his roots.

In *Cheap Day Return* Delderfield sets out to prove the superiority of small-town life over cosmopolitan living, and he fails. Neither in 1962 nor 1932 is Redcliffe Bay a truly attractive place in which to live. The latter is a pale copy of the rest of the Western world, fully connected to the trends and problems of the greater society, while the former is so bland, provincial, and mean as to be even less inviting and interesting than the community it developed into.

Cheap Day Return is a partial rewrite of *All Over the Town*, and it is not as successful a novel. Sandcombe is more complexly portrayed than is Redcliffe Bay. The mature Hearn is a fuller, rounder character than is Pip Stuart. The denizens of Sandcombe are more numerous, better sketched, and individualized. The activities of a local newspaper editor and his weekly play a role in both novels, but the depiction of editor and paper in the earlier novel is superior. Most of all, the nostalgia in *All Over the Town* is humorous and sweet. In *Cheap Day Return* it is bittersweet, undecided, and seemingly misplaced. It exudes a discontent that is external to the events of the story.

Come Home Charlie and Face Them

It is 1967 and again Delderfield has a man return to a seaside town where he spent a part of his youth. This time the man, Charlie Pritchard, is sixty-one years old and dying, the novel is a crime story, and the seaside town is in Wales. Again Delderfield employs the flashback. However, unlike in *The Spring Madness of Mr. Sermon*, Delderfield is not interested in presenting a nostalgic view of a seedy Welsh tin plate manufacturing town and seaside resort in 1929, nor is he as much interested in his crime plot, although it is, except for the climax, competently spun out; rather, the emphasis is on the maturation of Charlie, the twenty-three-year-old, timid, depressed, brow-beaten, and virginal bank clerk.

Charlie works for Cadwallader's Mercantile Bank in Penmadoc. He lives in the home of the bank's manager, Evan Rhys-Jones, Evan's wife, and their twenty-nine-year-old, spinsterish daughter, Ida, whom the Rhys-Joneses hope to match up with Charles. Ida is "two inches taller . . . and weighed half as much again"[6] as the five-foot

five-inch, 128-pound, bespectacled young teller. She is, however, a
level-headed, generous, and wise woman, who has no intention of
trapping Charlie. He finds her Rubenesque figure substantially gratifying as, in typical Delderfield style, she gives him manhood by
taking his virginity, stating, "A man of your age who has never had
fun with a woman wouldn't make much of a fist at walking out on a
safe job" (*CHCFT*, 30). Her motivation is generosity and the feeling
that she is helping a fellow human being. It was as if she were
saying: "Now this isn't going to hurt one little bit, Charlie. It'll be
over before you realize it" (*CHCFT*, 31).

Charlie's heart, however, is won by Delphine, the beautiful and
seemingly unattainable Italian waitress at the Rainbow Café. As the
reader later learns, Ida leaves town to have Charlie's baby, whom she
gives up for adoption, while Charlie is seduced by Delphine into
joining a plot to rob the bank via keys made from impressions and a
tunnel from the café to the nearby bank building.

Delphine lives and works with her "brother," Beppo, a swarthy
villain who later turns out to be her husband, but who may in fact
have been her brother also. Charlie's motivation for joining the plot,
which has been masterminded by the seemingly unintelligent Beppo,
is not greed but a desire for revenge on the officers of the bank who
have continually mistreated him, and the belief that overtakes him
that a man must rebel against the system that oppresses him, even to
the point of becoming an outlaw. Thirty-eight years later the dying
Charlie remains convinced he was right in plotting against the bank
in his youth. This is rather uncharacteristic of Delderfield, and the
author, after flirting with radicalism and political profundity, quickly
drops them and emphasizes his well-wrought plot.

The intriguers do well and Charlie becomes adept in the fabrica-
tion of the details of the burglary and the escape, which he hopes
will end in his marriage to the enticing Delphine. However, as they
are near to breaking into the bank, Charlie secretly witnesses
Delphine and Beppo having sex and he realizes that she has only used
him. Finding their passport and rail tickets, Charlie also realizes that
he is to be dumped after the heist.

They succeed in breaking into the bank and bringing the money
through the tunnel. Beppo then shoots at Charlie when Delphine
discovers that Charlie has taken their passport and tickets and is
obviously wise to the double-cross. Beppo misses and Charlie desper-
ately jumps on him from the stairs, accidentally killing him. Beppo

fires a shot as he dies but it accidentally hits Delphine and kills her too. Clearly the book's climax is not an example of Delderfield's best in plot construction, and this may suggest why he wrote no other crime story. He had rather typed himself into a corner.

With his coconspirators dead and all the incriminating evidence on his hands, Charlie is distraught. He is ready to give himself up, but fortunately for him Ida appears on the scene. She has just returned to town on a late train and passed the café where the noise of the covering sound from a player piano attracted her attention. She quickly takes over in order to save Charlie. They bury the bodies and the money at a construction site. Charlie is never found out. He marries Ida out of both gratitude, admiration for her cool-headedness, and genuine affection. He resumes his career in banking and rises to a managership. They have a good life together but Ida dies in her fifties. Learning that he has a terminal illness, Charlie returns to Penmadoc to relive the daring episode of his youth before he dies. To his great shock he finds that workmen are tearing up the asphalt under which is buried Delphine, Beppo, and the money.

Thirty-eight years before Delphine had first broached the idea of burglarizing the bank to Charlie by showing him a newspaper article about a successful robbery of a Scottish bank by one of its employees. The article was "Come Home Charlie and Face Them." That Charlie apparently never did. Charlie Pritchard has come home and, as he lives out his last few days, he writes an account of the theft to be found after death claims him.

Delderfield casts Charlie's story as first-person narrative. It is really his confession, the document he has begun to write at the end of the novel. The author has used this confessional form before, in *Farewell, the Tranquil Mind*, but it is employed more subtly here. *Come Home Charlie and Face Them* has a deliciousness about it precisely because it is the confession of a man who for one moment in his life took on the system and won. He kept no money. He did feel guilt that his innocent father-in-law suffered somewhat for his actions. However, he persevered, he endured, and he survived his danger with the result that he became more of a man because of his action. The bank robbery was Charlie's combat. It banished boredom from his life and it had a bittersweet ending. He was able to face the drab remainder of his working life because once in his youth he had been madly daring.

R. F. Delderfield's five shorter novels of the 1960s were interludes between and among the far longer and more intricate sagas. Clearly he enjoyed "dashing them off." For Delderfield a book of a mere 250 or so pages must have seemed like something of a warm-up exercise. Each is unique. Each presents a different challenge to the author: the comic novel, the satire, the historical novel, the nostalgic novel, and the crime novel. None of these works are profound or of lasting significance, but they provide the reader with much pleasure and considerable insight into the breadth and scope of Delderfield's narrative techniques and skills.

Chapter Six
A Horseman Triumphs

A Horseman Riding By is R. F. Delderfield's most typical family saga and his finest effort in that traditional form. It is a microcosm of English country life set against the background of British social, political, and military history from just after Queen Victoria's death to 1965. At center stage is Paul Craddock, a wounded veteran of the Boer War. He is surrounded by a swirl of some one hundred characters as the saga takes him from age twenty-three to his death at eighty-six. Minus the villainy he is a West Country Soames Forsyte, and *A Horseman Riding By* is a West Country *Forsyte Saga*. Like John Galsworthy's famous saga, this work weaves drama, violence, and sex around the double helix of family and history. The title is taken from the epitaph William Butler Yeats wrote for himself, "cast a cold eye / On life, on death. Horseman, pass by." Paul Craddock is the horseman and his long journey is the story. By means of it Delderfield instructs the reader to think of but not mourn the past. The future waits ahead for all.

Delderfield wrote *A Horseman Riding By* in three parts. *Long Summer Day* and *Post of Honour* were published together in 1966 as *A Horseman Riding By* and later published separately. *The Green Gauntlet*, the third part, was published in 1968. *A Horseman Riding By* was

also made into a successful BBC-TV series. The three volumes contain a total of over 1,700 pages. Although using the omniscient
narrator third-person point of view as the apex of his discourse,
Delderfield nevertheless focuses the story from Paul Craddock's perspective. There is little satire in the saga, but on an ironic, secondary
narrative level, the author savages the world of unenlightened
squirearchy, greedy developers, and wartime profiteers.

The heart of the saga is the ficticious Sorrel Valley located in
Devon on the coast and placed next to "Sennacharib" in *Diana*. In
fact, Diana's manor house, Heronslea, also figures in this saga, and
family names of characters in *A Horseman Riding By* are sometimes
also found in *Diana*. Delderfield has added another piece of geogra-
phy to his fictional Devon. The Sorrel Valley, like Sennacharib, is a
lovely place with almost magical powers to heal and renew, something akin to Shakespeare's Forest of Arden. The reader always sees
the valley through Paul Craddock's eyes. As he sits upon his horse he
surveys the world he has come to love:

At the top of the slope he reined in to give Snowdrop a breather, sitting
with his legs free of the stirrups and looking down through the straggle of
woods to the mere. The basin was full of violet dusk and the great clump of
oaks, immediately below, still showed traces of summer, like dowagers
clinging to the rags of finery. All the other trees, except the evergreens, had
surrendered to autumn and away to the west, where the woods ran down to
Home Farm pastures, the beeches stood like huge, bronze mushrooms,
marching through a shallow sea of green. Most of the hedgerow flowers
were gone but here and there, as a pledge of spring, was a stray campion
and on the very edge of the wood a few foxgloves, still standing sentinal
with bells ready to ring. As always, unless the wind was in the north he
could smell the sea here, and its tang reminded him of ventures past so that
he could isolate his purpose as never before.[1]

Despite war, economic crisis, social upheaval, and human failing,
Delderfield's beautiful countryside lives on. It is not that much of the
Sorrel Valley, and particularly his estate, Shallowford, belong to Paul.
It is that he belongs to the valley as do the many others living there:
the tenants, the wicked noblemen, the parsons, the poachers, the
merchants, the laborers, and even the real estate developers. All
belong to the Sorrel.

Long Summer Day

The years are 1902 to 1911. For those English who endured and
survived World War I the years immediately before 1914 seemed like
a long summer day. There was peace and prosperity. An unpopular
conflict, the Boer War, had ended. The British Empire, upon which
"the sun never set," seemed secure. Change was expected but it
would come, most people thought, through a gradual evolution.
Only the militant suffragettes were violently protesting the status
quo. Few foresaw the cataclysm of forthcoming war.

The period is also referred to by historians as the Edwardian
afternoon. It was dominated by the corpulent, fun-loving, good-
natured, and popular monarch, King Edward VII, whose coronation
in 1902 and death in 1910 serve as structural bastions in the novel,
as does the coronation of his son, King George V, in 1911. As uncle
to the German kaiser and Russian czar, Edward made general European peace a family matter. With his death began the unraveling of
European society that is still in progress today.

Long Summer Day opens in a London military hospital where cavalry Lieutenant Paul Craddock, twenty-three years old, is in grave
danger of dying from his poorly treated leg wound. An early weakness in the book is that the reader never learns much about Paul's
background except that his mother is dead, his father, a successful
cockney scrap metal dealer, has died while Paul was fighting in South
Africa, and that Paul attended a second-rate public school. His
father's former business partner, a Middle-European Jew named Franz
Zorndorff, arrives, notes the indifferent treatment Paul is receiving,
and sets about to save the young soldier through liberal doses of
money in the form of tips, bribes, and fees to specialists. Paul's leg is
operated on and he fully recovers except for being left with a lifelong
slight limp. Loyal to the memory of his ex-partner and growing fond
of Paul, Zorndorff becomes a surrogate uncle to the veteran.

Although a born Londoner himself, Paul dislikes the city and
despises the scrap yard in which his father earned a fortune. Unable
to continue in the army because of his handicap, Paul decides to
become a farmer, and Zorndorff takes an option on a huge estate in
Devon for him. It is more than Paul had wanted as a starter in
agriculture, but the young man, with an assured good income from
the scrap business behind him, journeys down to Shallowford, the

estate, and although he knows almost nothing about farming he buys it, for he has quickly fallen in love with the beautiful area. Paul is now the owner of a manor, several farms, much livestock; and he is responsible for his tenants, their families, and their hired laborers, some one hundred people. In others words, with a scratch of a pen he has become an instant squire.

Fortunately, the competent and honest estate manager, John Rudd, an ex-cavalryman himself and a generation older than Paul, agrees to stay on. Together they rebuild the estate, which has been allowed to run down due to the inattention of the previous, aristocratic owner, Sir George Lovell. However, it is many years before a profit is turned. Luckily, Paul has the supplemental income from his interest in the scrap yard, which Zorndorff wisely has refused to let Paul sell.

At the time Paul is about to purchase the estate, he meets Grace Lovell, a poorer cousin of the previous owner and daughter of the Lovell family ne'er-do-well and his first wife, whom he drove to suicide in India through his drinking and womanizing. Grace is beautiful, aristocratic, sure of herself, and enigmatic. The inexperienced Paul falls head over heels for her even though he has been ingenuously flirting with Claire Derwent, the attractive blonde daughter of his chief tenant. After giving a grand party for the entire estate in honor of the coronation of Edward VII, a party instigated and organized mainly by Claire, Paul proposes marriage to Grace, who after a while accepts, warning him, however, that she does not love him. Foolishly, Pauls believes he can win her heart as he has won her body. Claire is heartbroken, for she is deeply in love with Paul. She flees to London to live and work for several years.

Paul and Grace are basically incompatible although they work hard at their marriage at first. They have a son, Simon, but Paul is a conservative person, intrinsically if not politically. He wants no part of city life and he has dedicated himself to the welfare of his tenants and the growth and development of the estate. He resists the automobile and the telephone. Grace is cynical about men. She thinks: "All the men I met when I was capable of being hurt were so-called men of the world, who enjoyed putting the screw on women, but now that I have learned to give as good as I get all I meet are boys with men's bodies! There ought to be some kind of half-way house between these extremes but there isn't. One has to settle for one or the other" (*LSD*, 321). She is headstrong and a champion of women's rights, determined to fight for universal suffrage. Furthermore, she loves culture and travel and is not interested in farming. In fact, she takes no interest in any of Paul's professional or vocational pursuits.

While Paul is stumping for the local Liberal candidate for Parliament, Grace gets involved in a minor and completely innocent flirtation with the naval officer son of John Rudd. Paul tries to "control" Grace, and she leaves him and their son, never to return. Her destination is London where she becomes a front-line soldier in the often violent battle for the vote for women. She is imprisoned and brutalized.

Paul is heartsore, disconsolate, and embarrassed. He is unable to understand, along with most men of his time, how a woman could give up her home, her child, and a loving husband for street warfare in a cause that seemed both unnecessary and unnatural. Learning from Grace's mother that his wife is about to be released from prison, Paul goes up to London to meet her at the gate. He asks her to return but she refuses, telling him that she will make divorce easy for him and that she regrets the great wrong she did to him by marrying him without either love or commitment in her heart. Then she disappears again, and Paul returns in deep depression to the solace of Devon.

A shipwreck occurs off the Devon coast near Shallowford, and Paul leads the men of the community in a mostly successful rescue attempt in which he is seriously injured. Meanwhile, Paul's protégé, Ikey Palfrey, a cockney boy he has befriended and brought to the estate and whom he is now educating, goes to London to beg Grace to go back to his suffering patron. She wisely sets him on the trail of Claire Derwent, and a letter from Ikey brings Claire back to Devon, to Paul's bedside where she helps nurse him back to health.

Now Paul falls in love with Claire. They marry after his divorce, and she becomes the perfect wife for the squire. She is a farmer's daughter. She loves the valley. She is a fine mother to Simon and to the twin sons, Stephen and Andrew, who are born in 1908 and the daughter Mary born in 1910. Moreover, she is satisfied with her role in life.

Going up to London for the coronation of George V, Paul and Claire see Grace enmeshed in a suffragist–police battle where she is knocked down and about to be trampled. Paul rescues her, and she and Claire become friends. Grace returns to her comrades and Paul and Claire go back to Shallowford, Paul now convinced of the justice of Grace's cause.

As the novel draws to a close, Paul and Claire organize a coronation fête for the surrounding countryside at which Paul is called upon
at the last minute to enter a trap race. It is very dangerous, but he
and his horse and his rig emerge from the Ben Hur–like race safe
and victorious. At the end, the fête is cut short because of a great
storm that crosses the valley. It is symbolic of the coming war that
will draw a generation of young Englishmen into a cauldron of
death. But of lasting importance to Paul is his truth: that the Sorrel
Valley, "six miles wide and twelve deep," is the real England, and any
tiny piece of it "is more English than Trafalgar Square" (LSD, 557).
His wisdom, his good judgment of character, and his generosity have
counterbalanced and overcome Paul's inexperience with both women
and farming. He is as loved, admired, and accepted by the people of
the valley as if indeed he had been to the "manor" born.

Post of Honour

Post of Honour is a more exciting volume than Long Summer Day,
not because it covers a longer period of time—1911 to 1940—but
because the historical events of those years are the most traumatic
and devastating of the twentieth century: World War I, the Great
Depression, and the beginning of World War II. Once again
Delderfield uses coronations and deaths of the British monarchs as
the historical pylons around which he maneuvers his story: the coronation of George V, overlapping its celebration in Long Summer Day;
the silver jubilee of George V and Queen Mary; the death of George
V; Edward VIII's abdication so he could marry Mrs. Wallace Simpson
in 1936; and the coronation of George VI in 1937.

Paul Craddock's "vintage years" are those immediately before the
advent of World War I in August 1914, a time of peace, content-
ment, and prosperity which a little later "seemed as remote as the
Middle Ages."[2] Paul has evolved into a version of a tribal headman,
part mayor, part father figure, and part friend to the Sorrel Valley.
He and Claire are happy with their three children: the twins,
Stephen and Andrew born in 1908, and their daughter Mary born in
1910. They will have three more: Karen, born 1913; Claire, con-
ceived while Paul is on a brief leave from the Western front in 1917
and born in 1918; and the child of their second honeymoon, John,
born in 1934. Additionally, Claire loves Paul and Grace's son, Simon, now seven, as if he were her own.

With studied and pleasant ingenuousness, Paul's saga continues. Of course, it is also the saga of all the people of the Sorrel Valley. Paul's right-hand man, the agent John Rudd, has taken as his second wife, the valley's "Lady doctor," and Maureen, in her late thirties, gives birth to a son. In fact, couples are having babies all over the place, for the valley is something of a magical land of high fertility for humankind, beasts, and plants. Delderfield is skillful in *Post of Honour* with the device of weaving together all the life in the Sorrel Valley. Gulls observe the goings on in the various farms.

Reminiscent of John Masefield's long poem, "Reynard the Fox," Delderfield devotes a full section of a chapter to the exploits of the valley's oldest and wisest fox, Traveller, who has survived many a hunt and "who knew the valley and the valley folk far better than Paul Craddock and Smut Potter, better than Smut's gypsy mother" (*PH*, 402). Traveller is the animal kingdom correspondent to Paul. He is the four-footed master of the valley. He has aged with his human equivalent, and after surveying his domain on foot as Paul regularly does on horseback, "He was already tired and it was a long way from home and his need of vixens was less urgent than in the past" (*PH*, 407). Delderfield, the avid hunter, could not refrain from a tribute to his beloved adversary and game: the elusive and clever English fox.

Paul's protégé, Ikey, has gone out to India as a professional army officer without realizing that he has impregnated the young, fey, Gypsy woodsprite, Hazel Pascoe; and Paul's ex-wife, Grace, has dropped out of sight in the suffragist war. Delderfield begins to develop a villain in *Post of Honour*: Sydney Cosdall, the son one of Paul's tenant farmers who murdered his nagging wife and killed himself. Squire Paul helped the bright orphan when he was a terrified boy. But the boy grows up into a conniving solicitor trying to buy up all the valley land he can in order to turn it over to tacky, nonagricultural developments. Ultimately Paul and Sydney run against each other for Parliament. Paul, the Liberal candidate, is an underdog, but he nearly defeats the favorite Tory. However, Sydney is unable to capitalize on his Parliamentary seat, and a sex scandal ultimately brings him down. His villainy, treachery, ingratitude, and bad will toward the Craddocks turn out to be of small consequence, although Paul does lose part of a prosperous farm to the developers. These events, however, occur after the watershed event of *Post of Honour*.

World War I was surely the greatest catastrophe in modern British history. For Britons the casualty rate was far greater that in World War II. A generation of young British men was destroyed in that four-year meat grinder of a war. It has a profound affect on Paul and his valley. Eighteen young men from the Sorrel die in the war, and others at home also become war-related casualties. War hysteria and jingoism create another kind of casualty, the loss of justice, fair play, and reason on the part of many of the valley inhabitants as they are whipped up by anti-German propaganda to drive out of the valley a harmless old refugee scholar and his son, despite Paul's intervention on behalf of the German professor.

A near casualty of the war is Claire's virtue and her marriage to Paul. An army camp has been set up in the valley, and while Paul is busy and distracted by the need to adjust the estate to the wartime economy and manpower shortage, Claire is nearly seduced by the handsome young Lieutenant Aubrey Lane-Phelps, a professional ladies' man. Claire is nearly pushed over the brink to adultery by her false belief that Paul is having an affair with Hazel Pascoe, now Hazel Palfrey, for Ikey, having returned from India on his way to the Western Front, learned of the wild birth of his son, Rumble Patrick, in a cave and "done the right thing" by Hazel in marrying the girl, whom he genuinely loves. In fact, Paul has been bringing letters from Ikey to Hazel and reading them to the illiterate girl. Claire discovers the truth in time to avoid mistaken revenge, confesses her lack of trust, and implores Paul to whip her bare rump with his riding switch as penance and to relieve her guilt. Paul refuses to be "a wife beater" and merely slaps her once on the behind and all is forgiven. Straight- arrow Paul is never tempted to stray, not even when he later meets his former wife and first love, Grace, in romantic circumstances.

Cooly, Paul resists the growing enthusiasm for the war. As a wounded veteran of the Boer War, he is in a better position to know the truth about mortal combat than almost all the other men in the valley. Furthermore, he correctly believes the war to be futile and unnecessary. Eventually, however, in late 1916 he rejoins the army for a reason quite in keeping with his earned reputation for "slow, cud-chewing thought, and carefully weighted decisions" (PH 131). In Paul's decision to risk his life for a proposition he feels invalid— maintaining British hegemony and honor—Delderfield astutely portrays a special kind of decent male behavior, albeit a misplaced virtue. The valley is deeply infected with a deadly social disease: jingoism. Almost all the good, high-principled men have joined the colors. Left are the draft evaders, connivers, profiteers, and speculators. Paul believes that "the only place for an honest man now was along side chaps like Henry Pitts and Smug Potter" (*PH*, 152). Many men have joined bad causes for good reasons. Paul is wrong, of course. It would have been better to join those decent men who were conscientious objectors and who went to prison for their belief that World War I was immoral. But Paul is far too conservative and too social a person to make that choice. After the war he would realize how courageous and right the conscientious objectors were.

Despite his slightly lame leg, Paul is given a commission as lieutenant in the Transportation Corps. Soon he is in France leading columns of supply trucks into the front lines, a job not dissimilar to that of Lieutenant Frederick Henry in Ernest Hemingway's *Farewell to Arms* (1929), whose job was to convoy ambulances in and out of the front lines.

At home Claire manages the valley with the aid of John Rudd. Ikey's wife, Hazel, cannot understand why all the young men are away. In her anxiety for Ikey and her brothers her mind slips and she begins to set fire to the valley hay ricks to make beacons so the boys may find their way home from France. In her madness she runs in front of an army staff car on the road and is killed. She too is a war casualty. Her son, Rumble Patrick, is taken into the manor where he is raised and educated by Claire and Paul.

In France, in a miraculous coincidence, Paul meets Grace again. Before the war she did six terms in prison for the suffragist movement. When the war broke out she felt that as a woman the place for her was at the side of the wounded and suffering, while also believing correctly that the war would bring the political emancipation of women for which she had fought. First she volunteered for nursing duty in hospitals, and then chose ambulance driving at the front. Although she had not thought about sex for many years, there she began a series of sexual liaisons with doomed young soldiers, some of them ten or fifteen years younger than herself, giving them a little taste and brief memory of one of life's beautiful experiences which they would never otherwise have had a chance for.

The encounter between Paul and Grace takes place on a road to the front. Paul is struck by Grace's courage and dedication. They later enjoy a meal together in a brief lull in the war and they plan to meet once more when Paul returns from a supply mission. But Grace is killed in a German air raid while on an ambulance run to the front. Death from the air is a fate other Delderfield characters have suffered in *The Avenue Story* and *Diana*. Paul attends her funeral in a military cemetery. He has no residual bitterness for Grace, only admiration and the memory of his once overwhelming passion for her and the few years of happiness they had together.

With Paul in residence at the front, Delderfield is again able to exercise his great ability in combat description. At the 1918 Battle of St. Quentin

The pattern of the drumfire now resolved itself into a steady pounding of extreme back and front areas and only occasional shells, mostly gas, fell in the intermediate zone so that there was no alternative but to return to the battery site and await the arrival of trouble-spot engineers to clear the road. The men in the leading lorries had been killed outright, so unencumbered with wounded, they were able to turn and head back the way they had come, driving directly into the sheet of flame on the horizon. (*PH*, 269–70)

As always in Delderfield's writing the description of war is clear, precise, generally unemotional, and highly evocative of the event portrayed. The reader cannot fail to be moved, excited, fascinated, and horrified by his incisive descriptions.

In March 1918, during the final German offensive of the war, with the British in a retreat reminiscent of Hemingway's description of the Italian retreat in *A Farewell to Arms*, Paul is hit by shrapnel as he stops to help a wounded French soldier. The metal tears into his skull and he is left for dead. But the advancing Germans take him to a field hospital where a magnanimous brain surgeon saves his life. Paul recovers slowly and is repatriated with a silver plate in his head and headaches that will plague him for a long time.

At home at Shallowford, the valley heals him of his physical and mental wounds. As many surviving soldiers did after World War I, Paul plants a group of trees, one for each of the fallen men of the valley. He calls the tiny grove French wood, and he includes a tree for Grace and one for Hazel. His protégé, Ikey, who predicted the need for tanks to break the stalemate of the Western Front, and who proved their value to the old cavalry generals, has been killed in the final weeks of the war after surviving almost four years on the deadliest battlefield in human history.

The saga then jumps ahead ten years to September 1929 just before the financial crisis that led to the Great Depression. Paul is now fifty. His companion John Rudd, nearly eighty, goes to his reward. The children of Claire and Paul now come into full focus.

Paul begins to see the Shallowford estate in battle terms. The economic crisis is a kind of war on the homefront, and he must protect the estate from the abandonment of marginal farms, the encroachment of developers, and the drying up of his own funds. He successfully brings the estate through the depression, but there are grave personal difficulties for Paul even as the twins grow up and go into the scrap business with old Franz Zorndoff, Karen marries an Air Force officer, and Mary marries Rumble Patrick Palfrey, with whom she settles down to farm in the valley, much to Paul's delight. First Claire, at fifty, has unexpectedly become pregnant again. She is embarrassed, disappointed, and depressed, not wanting to tie up her life for so many more years with a child. A rift grows between husband and wife and they do not make love for six months. In Delderfield marriages frequent sex with gusto, good communication, and fidelity are the ingredients for success. A far greater disaster sends Claire and Paul back to each other's arms.

At sixteen, their daughter Claire has grown into a stunning beauty. She wins the local Dairy Queen contest and goes on to London where to the family's delight and pride she is selected British Dairy Queen of 1934. The new queen is sent with a British agricultural delegation to The Hague. On the way the plane she is flying on crashes at sea and the beautiful young girl is lost. Her memorial service in the valley is without a body to mourn. It is never recovered.

Slowly Paul and Claire overcome their loss. A world tragedy is brewing. Old Franz Zorndoff, now a nonagenerian, warns of another world war coming and then dies. Paul's son with Grace, Simon, has developed into a sensitive, socially conscious person. He has disagreed with his father politically, although there remains much love and respect between the two men. Simon is a radical socialist, and Paul, although very sensitive to the problems of the human condition, has always chosen to help a few individual people in a direct and personal way. It is a part of his Liberal party tradition and for Delderfield it is the correct way. When the Spanish Civil War breaks out in 1936 and Hitler and Mussolini send troops to help the fascists under Franco, Simon, against his father's advice, goes off to fight in

Spain for the Republicans. He is captured and imprisoned. Fortunately, Paul is able to pull a few political strings and get Simon out
of Spain. However, Paul now realizes that Simon is basically right.
Fascism will have to be stopped somewhere, someday, on some front.

War comes and all of the Craddock men go into uniform except
Paul, who is too old for active service. He realizes this war is
different from World War I. The cause is just. The very civilization
is at stake. Paul and Claire battle on the homefront by producing
food. Thanks to old Zorndoff's warning the estate is fueled, stocked,
and ready for the siege of war. Simon is the first to see action and
appears to be lost after the retreat from Dunkirk, so that Paul begins
to grieve for the loss of his firstborn. But Simon is as tough and as
plucky as his mother was. Delderfield always feels that a person's
genes form his or her character. Simon dives into the channel as the
German army reaches him, finds a floating oil can, and swims until
he is rescued by a destroyer. Claire had made an excellent swimmer
out of her stepson years ago, and thus made possible his escape.

In 1940, with modern warfare raging on land, sea, and sky, and
under the sea, Paul is still shaving with his Boer War straight razor.
He has grown into a crusty middle-aged squire. With the German
invasion seemingly imminent, Paul joins other middle-aged and old
men armed with shotguns and 22-calibre rifles in the Local Defence
Volunteers organized by Winston Churchill. But though the outlook
for the British is grim as they face the German onslaught all alone,
Paul is not despondent as *Post of Honour* comes to an end. He has
faith in the strength and courage of the younger generation, and he
will not find them lacking.

Now in his sixties, Paul Craddock has become more tolerant, more
wise, more forgiving, and more patient, with the passing years. His
generosity and wisdom in dealing with his tenants have worked out
to the benefit of all. His love for the land has continued to grow, and
he never truly regretted his decision to settle in and develop the
Shallowford estate in the Sorrel Valley. Delderfield's great love for his
Devon home county has been transferred to his finest literary surrogate, Squire Paul Craddock, once of London and now of Devonshire.
But *A Horseman Riding By* is only two thirds over.

The Green Gauntlet

The Green Gauntlet turns *A Horseman Riding By* into a three decker,
an ancient and honorable tradition in the history of the English

novel. This volume is itself divided into two titled parts: "Part One—The Beleaguered" and "Part Two—Conditional Surrender." Furthermore, for the first time in *A Horseman Riding By*, Delderfield gives each chapter a title, and almost of all of them are war references such as "Hit and Run," "Garrison Duty," "Ration Party," "Long Range Salvo," "Booby Trap," "Marchout with Banners," "Routine Reconaissance," "Counter Attack," and "Terms of Capitulation." These military terms symbolize Paul Craddock's personal war with all the forces ranged in opposition to his attempt to keep Shallowford and the Sorrel Valley from those adversaries—political, social, military, and natural—which would alter his beloved feudal fiefdom in the last twenty three years of his long life, from 1942 to 1965.

The book is called *The Green Gauntlet* first because in the beginning the valley is "seen" by a crippled gull flying over the territory as "a great gauntlet, a green and russet gauntlet of the kind falconers used centuries ago."[3] And the gauntlet, symbol too of British defiance, has been flung down in challenge to the Germans once more. Later the valley is again compared to a green gauntlet when John, Claire's and Paul's last child, uses a television production to save a significant portion of the estate woods from being cut down for an airport expansion. The show is titled "The Green Gauntlet" because it was noticed during an aerial survey: "This Valley, from a thousand feet, looks like a gauntlet . . . a great, finger-spread glove made of green and rust-colored leather" (*GG*, 406). Now, in the 1950s, the gauntlet is flung down against developers, speculators, and big government.

All of part 1 is devoted to World War II. Thus a three-year period in Paul's, the valley's, and Britain's life is given well over half of the book's pages. By comparison, World War I receives slightly less than half of the pages in *Post of Honour*. Clearly the two wars are the central events of *A Horseman Passing By*.

The Green Gauntlet begins slowly, perhaps reflecting the slower pace of the war in early 1942. Expectedly, the focus of the novel shifts to the Craddock children, who will all be involved in the war. Again Delderfield employs a dastardly German air raid to advance his plot. In February 1942 stray German raiders drop six bombs on the estate. It is as if Germany has declared war specifically on the valley. In the raid Simon's wife, Rachel, who shared his radicalism but no longer his bed, is killed. Meanwhile, besides Simon, the twins, Stevie and Andy, have joined up, Daren, whom all call Whiz, is with her R.A.F. husband in the Far East, while Mary and her husband,

Rumble Patrick, have had their farmhouse destroyed in the same raid
that killed Rachel. Rumble decides to join the merchant marine
instead of rebuilding their farm. Paul attempts to dissuade him, and
there is a typical Delderfield exchange in which participation in
World War II is justified. Paul naturally points out the importance of
agriculture to a nation blockaded by submarines. Rumble, speaking
this time for Delderfield, replies that the only way he can justify
having a part of postwar Britain is to fight for it. Those who do are
entitled to what they have risked their lives to save. Paul is forced to
agree.

At sixty-two, Paul is too old to serve in the combat army. Instead,
he is serving in the Local Defence Volunteers to defend the coast
against the imminent German invasion that was thwarted by the
Battle of Britain. The force becomes the Home Guard for the dura-
tion. Paul's major contributions to the war are his successes in orga-
nizing valley agriculture and giving his three sons to the military
effort, one of whom is killed and one badly wounded. John, born in
1934, is too young to soldier.

The central soap opera of *The Green Gauntlet* is the relationship
among the twins and their wives. Like Bernie and Boxer in *The
Avenue Story*, Stevie and Andy are remote and different from their
father and they are devil-may-cares. Stevie has married Monica, a
selfish, upwardly mobile parson's daughter, while Andy has married
Margy, a down-to-earth Welsh nurse. At the outbreak of war both
men become R.A.F pilots, Andy in fighters operating out of Egypt,
and Stevie in the Bomber Command, attacking Germany from
British bases. Monica cannot understand Stevie's patriotism and sense
of duty and tries to pull strings to get him out of the service. He
refuses, and she leaves him. He turns to Margy, who is nursing in
London, while her husband is overseas, for advice. Her marriage has
not been good either and with Andy so long gone, she has been
having affairs. Desperate for love and caring, she seduces the emotionally wounded Stevie, and a long love affair commences with the
result that Margy becomes pregnant. Andy is shot down in the
Western Desert of Egypt and presumed dead, so Stevie plans to
divorce Monica and marry Margy. Of course, neither Claire nor Paul
know anything about these happenings.

In another fine Delderfield plot twist, those old flying deus ex
"machines" step in and it is learned that Andy is not dead. He has
been badly wounded and has lost an arm and a part of his face has

been burned away. Meanwhile, Claire has finally learned of the mess that threatens to destroy her family and she takes courageous action worthy of a Craddock. She goes to Stevie's airbase to make him give up the relationship until Andy returns, has healed somewhat, and has a chance to make some decisions of his own. She does not want Andy to know that Margy's child is his brother's. Alas, as Claire arrives at the airbase she learns that Stevie has been killed, crash-landing his stricken bomber. He could have saved his own life by parachuting out, but he chose to stay with his plane to save his wounded rear-gunner.

Claire rushes to Margy, of whom she is genuinely fond, and asks her to come to the estate to wait for Andy and give him a chance to deal with the unexpected emotional blow. He, however, is so numbed and warped by his experience that he is not angered by Margy and Stevie's betrayal. Rather, he is indifferent to her, but he welcomes the child, Vanessa, as the replacement love for the love which he had for his brother. The marriage resumes but it is strained and without affection, except for the love of the child. Margy hangs on for a while out of guilt.

There are no more Craddock war casualties. In fact, the valley, like Britain itself, is not decimated of young men in the way it was by World War I. Only a few men and women are killed, and there is no need for a second French Wood memorial.

In *The Green Gauntlet* Claire develops as she matures. She moves beyond being Paul's bedmate and household manager and becomes a resourceful and brave woman. In one incident she shows her physical courage when she helps thwart the escape of a dangerous, armed German prisoner of war. Paul remains very much turned on by Claire's beauty and voluptuousness, and they maintain an active and healthy sex life throughout middle age and into old age. Chauvinistically, he used to think of her "as someone who was always a lot of fun horizontally but only adequate when you were vertical" (*GG*, 255). Now he admires her handling of the several physical and emotional dangers that have threatened them and those whom they love. Claire's finest hour is yet to come, however.

In 1955, when she is seventy-two, Claire learns that she has angina and may not live long. She keeps her illness secret from everyone. When a valley disaster takes place and the Sorrel floods, she is trapped with Vanessa in Margy's ruined cottage. Claire saves her granddaughter's life at the cost of her own. The last words she

hears, as her heart gives out and she is swept away, are the shouts of
Paul, ever in charge in emergencies and coming to her rescue. Claire,
who always seemed a little shallow and a little selfish, who did not
mourn for her son Stevie because all of her love was directed to her
husband, becomes in the end a forceful person of heroic stature and
ultimate generosity.

After the war, when Paul is sixty-six, he makes the greatest business error of his career. In order to compensate Andy for his sacrifice
and suffering, to distribute power among his children, and to avoid
ruinous death taxes when he should die, Paul forms a corporation of
the estate with voting shares going to each of his children as well as
himself. Meanwhile, Andy, in partnership with a fellow wounded
veteran named Shawcrosse who becomes the villain-developer replacing Sydney Cosdall, plots to turn part of the estate into a trailer park
and eventually cut up the entire estate after getting control from the
family. Margy discovers the plot and out of loyalty to her in-laws
reveals it to the Craddocks. Andy is foiled although, as he predicts,
the encroachments continue.

Ostracized, Andy goes into self-exile in America for five years after
Margy takes Vanessa and leaves him. He returns when he learns that
his mother has died, partly as a result of the flood that valley
development, in cutting acres of trees, had caused. He forces
Shawcrosse to sell him a farm they had manipulated out of the
Shallowford estate. Andy then gives the farm back to Paul. Father
and son reconcile, and there is also a reconciliation between Margy
and Andy, who now goes into the antiques business.

All further attempts to destroy Shallowford are fended off. In
1959, at the age of eighty, Paul, who was once called Young Squire,
then Squire, is now referred to as Old Squire. Simon, having survived innumerable battles and skirmishes, has remarried happily and
found his vocation as a schoolmaster, giving up radical politics and
moving toward Paul's and Delderfield's Liberal position. Paul meanwhile has shifted a little to the Left, recognizing that Simon was
right in fighting the fascists in Spain and right in battling for more
equal opportunity at home.

As Paul moves well into his healthy eighties, only bothered by a
little bronchitis brought about because he refuses to give up smok-
ing, he misses Claire more and more: "He was filled with a great
longing to see Claire, to reach out and touch her, to hear her voice
and catch the sparkle of her eye as she looked over her shoulder at

him while tugging a comb through her hair . . . " (*GG*, 504).
Earlier in *A Horseman Riding By* the great national occasions are
enthusiastically or solemnly celebrated in the valley, but after World
War II such commemorations are muted. V-E Day in 1945 cannot
compare to Armistice Day 1918. The coronation of Queen Elizabeth
II in 1952 is hardly noted. Finally, an occasion arises that truly stirs
Paul. Winston Churchill dies in 1965 and Paul, nearly eighty-six,
nevertheless goes up to London to pay his respects at the funeral, for
he feels that Churchill was the living embodiment of the best of his
own era. Paul wears his seven medals from his three wars: the Boer
War, World War I, and those he received for his service in the Home
Guard during World War II.

Returning home to Shallowford he reaches his eighty-sixth birthday and senses that his life is quickly drawing to a close. Almost
daily he asks Rumble Patrick to take him up into the woods in the
Land Rover. Finally, one bright summer day, he sees the Sorrel and
the valley in its pristine glory for the last time. A bronchial seizure
takes him and the old soldier surrenders at last, his white handker-
chief fluttering from his hand like a flag of truce. His last memory is
of the rich aroma of all the life around him: "the tang of gorse, the
resin of the pines, the smell of turned soil that would bring gulls
flocking, and, behind all these, the sharp, healing whiff of the sea"
(*GG*, 507). A last lone gull flies overhead like an aerial salute to a
dead hero. This final chapter of *The Green Gauntlet* is among
Delderfield's finest writing, comparable to John Galsworthy's description of the placid death of Old Jolyon in "The Indian Summer of a
Forsyte" (1918).

Paul Craddock, a symbol of what is traditionally best in British
manhood, had a special destiny, and he fulfilled that destiny. It was
to give his sweat, his blood, some of his children, and his fortune to
saving a beautiful English locale so that it would remain both a
productive and efficient provider of food for the nation's stomach, and
a refuge for wild nature providing peace and succor for the nation's
soul. He preserved a space for the spirit of Old England in one of its
finest valleys, where in a way he and Claire reigned there as an
ancient god and goddess commanding their temple and their grove.
Simon inherits the estate and the care of the valley. It is in good
hands. Furthermore, Paul and Claire and Grace have left twenty-
seven grandchildren to help out both valley and country if there
should be future need. And the great-grandchildren are on the way.

96   R. F. DELDERFIELD

The Sorrel Valley is R. F. Delderfield's microcosm of Britain. Paul is the Churchill surrogate. Were it not for the integrity of many Pauls, implies Delderfield, the great saving work of Winston Churchill would have been in vain. *A Horseman Riding By* is R. F. Delderfield's elaborate tribute to the region and the nation he truly loved. Although he has his alter ego Paul grouse about the encroachment of unwise and unthought-out development, about mindless governmental interference in the daily life of ordinary citizens, and about the stupidity of most but not all politicians, nevertheless, in the final analysis, there is great love expressed for a place and a people, warts and all. *A Horseman Riding By* is a novel of time, of family, of character, and of change. It is not likely that the reader, once he or she picks it up, will be able to lay it aside unfinished. The diorama of Devon is memorable; the cast is unforgettable.

Chapter Seven
Swann Song

Within the last four years of his life R. F. Delderfield wrote *To Serve Them All My Days* (1972) and the first three volumes of what was tentatively projected as a five-volume saga of the Swann family: *God Is an Englishman* (1970), *Theirs Was the Kingdom* (1971), and *Give Us This Day* (1973), some 2,800 pages of good writing, a prodigious accomplishment for any writer, well or ill.

To Serve Them All My Days

To Serve Them All My Days, a one-volume miniepic, the story of twenty-three years in the life of a schoolmaster named David Powlett-Jones, is Delderfield's most popular, most critically successful, and most artistically accomplished single volume effort. It was the subject of a successful BBC-TV series and was shown in America as part of Public Television's Masterpiece Theater. Delderfield wrote it, however, to take a break from the rigorous demands of pounding out the Swann saga books and to pay homage to an educational system he admired—the public boarding school—and an institution he loved—West Buckland School in Devonshire. In the preface to *To Serve Them All My Days* Delderfield hints that one of the six schools he attended as a youth, he could "still regard with the greatest affection."[1] Since West Buckland was the only boarding school he attended, and since it is in rural Devon, it must be the model for the novel.

Delderfield had paid homage previously to West Buckland when in 1963 he edited and introduced *Tales Out of School: An Anthology of West Buckland Reminiscences, 1895–1963*. In that work Delderfield relates several experiences that are later fictionalized in *To Serve Them All My Days*. He revered Ernie Harries, the Headmaster of West Buckland for more than thirty years (*TOS*, 25). The jovial, kind-hearted, and astute father figure of a headmaster in *To Serve Them All My Days* is named Algernon Herries. For Delderfield the schoolmaster who "taught me to wander very happily in the garden of English literature" was Sam Howells (*TOS*, 25). In the novel David Powlett-Jones's best friend is Howarth, the wise, the acerbic, chain-smoking English master. In *For My Own Amusement* Delderfield described Sam Howells as the man who pointed out to him the path to culture "and that path was clearly signposted" by the great writers of history (*FMOA*, 1968, 139). Sam Howells introduced Delderfield to the craft of literature, and Delderfield in return memorialized him, as well as Headmaster Harries, in *To Serve Them All My Days*.

Two earlier novels influenced *To Serve Them All My Days*. The first is the classic story of English public boarding school life, Thomas Hughes's *Tom Brown's School Days* (1857). In this novel the real-life educational theorist, Thomas Arnold, master of Rugby School and father of the poet Matthew Arnold, is presented as the ideal head-master. Arnold reformed public school education by eschewing gross corporal punishment, diverting the traditional war between masters and boys, and through personal example of rectitude by which means he turned the older boys of Rugby away from brutalizing and ex-ploiting the younger boys and toward his view of the true value of education: the development of character and physical fitness. Arnold extended the concept of "muscular Christianity" to the public school and in the process raised a second-rate school to the first rank of moral leadership. As David Powlett-Jones points out, Bamfylde "has always been second grade. Academically and socially, that is. Not in any other way."[2] Algy Herries and David Powlett-Jones are, master and disciple, followers of Arnoldian education theory, as apparently is Delderfield. The author describes Herries's theories as "refurbished Arnoldian concepts" (*TST*, 191) and his followers like David as

"Progressive-traditionalists" (*TST*, 191). For them education is "a search for truth. Not simply truth about the universe but about us— ourselves. To see things and ourselves as they and we really are, not as fashionable trends and fashions project them, generation by generation . . . but you can't begin searching out truth until you know yourself, and getting to know yourself demands a reasonable amount of self-discipline" (*TST*, 240). And ultimately in the heat of argument David is always ready to say: "Go and read *Tom Brown* and see what the old Squire had to say about it" (*TST*, 510).

The second novel influencing *To Serve Them All My Days* is James Hilton's sentimental classic, *Goodbye, Mr. Chips* (1933), the story of an English public school master and his long relationship with a school called Brookfield. Hilton's story progresses up to and through World War I when, with tears in his eyes, the school master reads the roll call of the dead just as Herries does for Bamfylde's old boys in that war and David does for the dead of World War II. The parallels between *Goodbye, Mr. Chips* and *To Serve Them All My Days* are many. Chips marries late in life. David has a later second marriage. The schools involved are similar institutions. Both David and Chips lose wives tragically. Both are deeply and irrevocably in love with their schools. They serve gladly as *in loco parentis*. They remember all the names of their students long after they have gone. And they are loved by those they teach.

However, *To Serve Them All My Days* is much more than some "chips" off the old block. Whereas Hilton presents boarding-school life as a pastoral, soporific experience, Delderfield delves into educational politics, and David, nick-named Pow-Pow by the students, becomes a canny and competent academic trench fighter, as good as he was in three years of trench warfare on the Western Front. Delderfield goes beyond the sentimental character sketch of *Goodbye, Mr. Chips* to make points concerning the meaning of education and its relationship to political, spiritual, and material life. He is commenting on the nature of the British national character as it is molded in, and as it emerges from, the system of education that trains and has trained its leaders.

To Serve Them All My Days opens in early 1918 with twenty-year-old Second Lieutenant David Powlett-Jones of the South Wales Borderers arriving at Bamfylde school, a typical English boarding school for boys nine to nineteen. David, the son of a Welsh coal miner killed years before in a mine cave-in, is on sick leave from the Army hospital where he is being treated for shell shock and is seeking a teaching position at Bamfylde prior to medical discharge. He is not qualified for the position because he did not have time to get his university degree before the war. Also he is extremely nervous and depressed. However, there is a desperate manpower shortage and Headmaster Herries hires him, sensing that David could prove to be a teacher with a true avocation. As in all things academic, he proves right.

As perhaps all young teachers are, David is a bridge to the generations. His wartime experience separates him from the older teachers and makes him especially compassionate and caring for the boys who will shortly face the horrors of war as he did.

Fortunately, the war soon ends, and David, healed by the good air and the calm, eternal ways of Delderfield's beloved Devon, is allowed to stay on and earn his degree in history through a university extension program. Two years later, his previously nonexistent personal life commences when on a vacation in Wales he meets Elizabeth Marwood, a nineteen-year-old nurse from London. They quickly fall in love; he proposes marriage and is accepted. She is happy too at Bamfylde and soon she gives birth to twin daughters, Joan and Grace. As has been seen, twins run in Delderfield families.

Shortly afterward, there is a disastrous fire in one of the school dormitories and David heroically risks his life to rescue two trapped boys. As an aftermath of the experience and the acclaim, David realizes that he can never leave Bamfylde. His love for the place that healed his psychic wounds and offered him a happy haven for his family is in his blood forever. Even the tragic death of Beth and Joan in an automobile accident cannot shake that love and faith. After overcoming this second great emotional wound of his life, he resolves to carry on with his surviving but injured daughter, whom he nurses back to an almost full recovery.

In 1925 David begins writing a historical study of the life of Margaret of Anjou, wife of England's medieval King Henry VI. It will be six years before he finishes and it is published, but the work is solace in stressful times, and its success later gives him pleasure and prestige, although Delderfield treats literary fame like his own with derision when he has David realize that the reviewer who gave him a rave in the *London Times* is a distinguished historian and yet he had to look his name up: "So much for chaps who write books . . . I didn't even remember the author's name" (*TST*, 408).

When the General Strike of 1926 takes place, David's sympathies are clearly with the strikers. In London at the commencement of the strike, he hitchhikes and tramps his way back to Bamfylde to make sure the strikers' views are presented in the faculty and school debates. He has a brief love affair with the beautiful Julia Darbyshire, a former schoolmistress at Bamfylde, but she deserts David for marriage to a wealthy American just as he is deeply involved in his greatest academic struggle.

From his arrival at Bamfylde David had found himself in conflict with Carter, a science master and head of the R.O.T.C. despite the fact that he had avoided combat in the war. They battle over school philosophy, tradition versus progress, and Carter's jingoism. When Herries retires, both Powlett-Jones and Carter apply for the position despite the fact that both are young and not experienced enough for the job. The board of governors, in part to keep both teachers on the staff, appoint an older man to the headmastership. Alcock, the new head, turns out to be a hard-hearted, humorless, destructive martinet, who is determined to drive out the old staff, deemphasize character building and sports, and turn the school into a grind for university acceptance. Carter leaves, but David is determined to fight on. Julia's marriage and Alcock's attack come simultaneously and David feels doubly betrayed. Fortunately, he has his writing to retreat too. Finally, David secures Herries's help and counterattacks by sending his just grievances to the board. After a suspenseful period, the board decides in David's favor and admonishes Alcock, who it turns out was a man with a secret heart condition, and who in pique and frustration dies of heart failure as he is writing his letter of resignation.

The timely death of Alcock saves Bamfylde, rescues David, and makes it possible for him to be appointed headmaster at thirty-five. Now he can reinstall the Arnoldian-Herriesian academic philosophy. The school prospers and grows under David's wise leadership despite the Great Depression. Meanwhile, David has met and fallen in love with another woman, Christine Forster, a radical politician unhappily married to a Roman Catholic who refuses to allow a divorce. After two unsuccessful campaigns and some overseas studies, Christine is able to obtain a divorce, marry David, and settle uncomfortably at Bamfylde. It is much harder for her to adjust to the quiet academic life than it was for Beth. A stillborn child makes things worse, Christine goes into depression, and she runs away. The ever sympathetic and understanding David finds her, brings her back, and solves her problems by giving her a teaching position in the school and getting her pregnant again. A son is born and Chris is maternally fulfilled, Delderfield style, as David observes, "Why the devil did she ever bother with politics? This is what she really wanted. Maybe it'll take some of the steam out of her and that can't be a bad thing" (*TST*, 568).

As their son is born, David and Chris lose their good friend Howarth to lung cancer. He leaves a generous legacy to Bamfylde that is much needed and appreciated. Simultaneously, David hears from Julia after ten years. Her husband has died, and she is sending her son, Charles, to Bamfylde. He turns out to be a bright and popular lad, nicknamed Clark because he sounds like Clark Gable to his school chums. Two years later, in 1940, David receives a last letter from Julia telling him that she is dying of breast cancer and that Charles is his son, the result of their last, parting tryst. One must wonder why hardly any Delderfield couple, young or mature, married or otherwise, seems to have heard of birth control?

David decides not to tell anyone about Charles, but he is pleased to see that the boy has started life well. In 1941, with the war raging, David loses many of his staff to the services and the death roll commences again. He needs replacement teachers, and a wounded ex-soldier, wan, shaken, not academically qualified for teaching, comes to him for a position. The situation, as David realizes, is parallel to his first coming to Bamfylde, and like Herries before him, David welcomes, soothes, and hires the young veteran. The book ends with assurance that Bamfylde like Britain herself will endure and survive, and that David Powlett-Jones will work out his days the beloved headmaster, building character and body for the nation's future.

The great strengths of *To Serve Them All My Days* are the towering character of David Powlett-Jones and the atmosphere of Bamfylde. David develops and matures from a callow, broken youth into a man of sympathy, intelligence, courage, and integrity. His youthful political radicalism is tempered by experience and insight so that he grows into a person of tolerance for all ranks and respect for all views. And from the beginning to the end he is a just person—a man of principle. Bamfylde is stroked onto the pages of the novel with such precision and care that not only the bricks and beams of the institution stand out in bold relief, but the very sounds and smells seem real.

To Serve Them All My Days is ultimately a successful, sentimental projection of what Delderfield and his public would like boarding-school education to be. It is an idealization and a model. For all its realism and historical background, the novel is seen through a tinted lens that reduces the sharpness of the actual reality of a system of education and a complex period of history. Regardless, the sense of place, the astute characterization, and the author's obvious love of the project, place *To Serve Them All My Days* in the forefront of all of Delderfield's single volume works.

The Swann Saga

It was to have been his magnum opus, the longest work of a writer of long works. But he never finished it. Delderfield's plan was to write the history of an English commercial family as he had written the saga of an English agricultural family in *A Horseman Riding By*. As with the earlier work, the Swann saga was to combine the epic family novel with historical fiction. The period involved was to stretch from 1857 to the 1960s and require five volumes to complete. Only three volumes were completed, however, and the story only reached 1914.

At first glance the subject seems an unlikely one: the founding and history of a transportation company, Swann-on-Wheels, against the background of the development of British trade. Few English novelists have made heroes of men who gave up careers in the army in order to make money in business. That challenge is part of the reason for the existence of the Swann saga. The other main reason is that as he grew older Delderfield became more and more convinced of the rectitude and efficacy of the old Liberal party middle way that placed enlightened business management as the center of a just society. Capitalistic incentive could both create growth and provide fairly for the workers who produce the source of wealth. As Adam Swann, Delderfield's businessman hero, muses at the end of *God Is an Englishman*, his business and those of his compatriots "were dedicated to the making of money certainly, but it had a deeper, broader significance. You could, if you wished, regard it as a staging-post between a whole range of extremes— progress and *laissez-faire*, splendor and squalor, ignorance and expertise, affluence and grinding poverty."[3] That Delderfield could make high romance and popular success out of this unusual material and out-of-vogue political view is a tribute to his consummate skill as a storyteller and his ever-developing ability to create believable and interesting characters, a huge gallery of them in the Swann saga.

God Is an Englishman. *God Is an Englishman* is built consciously and serenely on literary clichés almost as old as *Gilgamesh*: stock situations and stock characters like a brave and honest soldier-hero, beautiful heroines, impeding and supporting parents, a scheming housekeeper, diligent urchins, a godly foreman, a Scottish sharper, a villainous rake, an upright bookkeeper, a repentant thief, and others. Delderfield's model is clearly Charles Dickens, whom, so that the reader cannot fail to get the point, Delderfield introduces as a character in the story, when after the hero Adam Swann has mentioned Dickens's work to his wife Henrietta, they see him on the train journey that is the climax of the book, a journey in which a wreck nearly ends Adam's life. Delderfield studied Dickens's life as well as his work, for the Victorian novelist was actually involved in a train wreck, the Staplehurst Railway disaster in 1866, in which Dickens acted as heroically and in much the same manner as does Adam Swann.[4] Although Delderfield cannot come near Dickens's depth and range of imaginative fiction, he is nevertheless able to approach the master in the area of the sketch that is part caricature and which takes on the simultaneous values of symbolization of type and commentary on the subject's nature.

In *God Is an Englishman* a new British Empire is to be conquered, and that empire is the world of business. The years of the war of commerce covered in this volume are 1857 to 1866. The book's shocking title (for anyone not English) is neither an expression of arrogance nor irony. After a long stay in Europe Swann sees at a French seaport a quay loaded with English manufactured goods. The English are winning the world with their manufacture. He muses: "God is an Englishman, sure enough!" (*GIE*, 660). It is a sentiment, a nineteenth-century insular English view of a universe where the sun never set on British soil, where God is decent, fair, just, straight-dealing, neat, reticent, orderly, and always a winner. That is, an Englishman.

The Englishman who is the hero of the novel is Adam Swann, an army lieutenant in the Indian service, a survivor of the charge of the

Light Brigade in the Crimean War and the Sepoy Mutiny in India, who is disgusted with the brutality of war and the stupidity of his superiors. He is slightly wounded in a skirmish with native troops and has the good fortune to find a precious ruby necklace on the body of a dead Indian mutineer. Once again, as in *A Horseman Riding By*, Delderfield begins an epic with a wounded soldier.

Adam is of a family of military gentry that has served England for six generations. His father, the colonel, was wounded at Waterloo. Adam, now thirty-one, decides, however, to leave the army and found a business fortune on the jewels. He says good-bye to his best friend, Lieutenant Roberts, the real-life Frederick Roberts who became Queen Victoria's greatest general and whom Delderfield brings back in *Theirs Was the Kingdom*.

Arriving home in England he is advised by a wise railway official to make use of his knowledge of horses, garnered in thirteen years of cavalry service, to go into the hauling and carting business to supplement the service of the railroad gridiron that has left many areas out of touch with the faster transport. Adam sets out to ride across country on horseback in order to see the situation for himself, and he confirms the official's estimate of potential business.

The long journey takes him into Lancashire, where near Manchester he sees the two Englands. First he sees the new England, the industrial towns where "The water in the streams about them turned grey and then black while the current, always sluggish, ceased almost to move" (*GIE*, 24). Through this country weaved the railway engine: "The drifting grime he exhaled could be seen in the form of a gigantic mushroom, silvery grey and dun brown by day, jet black, shot with crimson, by night" (*GIE*, 24). The old England lies below: "To the south, however, it was otherwise. Here the greater part of the Cheshire plain was green and gold, dotted with half-timbered farmhouses and neat rows of cottages linked by dust roads still bounded by hedges of hawthorn, elderberry and nodding cow-parsley. Cattle grazed here and nearby flocks of white geese strutted in charge of strident, red-cheeked children" (*GIE*, 24). Adam senses that he is destined to link the two nations together, although as a country man he is revolted by the living conditions for the proletariat in the satanic mills where "at least half the men and women—seemed to be twisted or crippled, as though he had strayed into the world of the brothers Grimm, populated by the humpbacked, the lame, and the knock-kneed" (*GIE*, 73).

Adam witnesses the murder of a child by a cruel mill owner in a
strikers' riot. The vicious capitalist is Sam Rawlinson, a living essay
on greed and misuse of labor. His beautiful daughter, Henrietta, is
being forced into an unwanted marriage and runs away from home.
Abandoned on the road, she is rescued by the passing Adam, who
takes her up behind him on his horse and spirits her away to his
father's home. They ride pillion through the countryside like a
knight errant and a damsel in distress.

Henrietta is safe at Adam's home, and when her raging father
comes to collect her, Adam defeats him by revealing his knowledge of
the murder, threatening to expose Rawlinson, and telling the father
it is his intention to marry Henrietta. She is surprised and delighted
for she has fallen in love with this real man, so different from the
man her father chose for her, Makepeace Goldthorpe, the wimpy
scion of a land-owning family. An allegory of class conflict has been
set up. Henrietta, although desiring to escape the greasy clutches of
Makepeace, nevertheless despises her father's humble background and
the business source of his wealth. She aspires to the life of the gentry
just as the man she will marry is determined to make his mark in the
commercial world.

Adam takes his jewels to an old army buddy in London, Josh
Avery, a disreputable gambler and man-about-town who has the
proper connections to fence the jewels. Instead of selling the jewels
for Adam, Josh asks and is accepted as a silent partner in the hauling
business Adam is about to start and which Henrietta has named and
for which she has created a logo of a swan on wheels, thus Swann-on-
Wheels. Josh remains a loyal friend until later in the story he falls
prey to the Spanish dancer, Esmeralda, who milks him of all his and
Swann's capital and then is murdered by her jealous dance partner,
whom Avery then kills. Adam, ever loyal, helps his weak friend to
escape, takes charge of the life of Avery's illegitimate daughter, and
struggles to survive without necessary capital.

Meanwhile Henrietta and Adam have married and have settled
down just outside of London in the environs of Croyden, familiar to
Delderfield readers as the locale for *The Avenue Story*. There they first
rent and then purchase a country estate called "Tryst." Like Paul
Craddock in *A Horseman Riding By*, Adam buys into a feudal manor
and estate. Henrietta is unequipped to handle the responsibility of
managing the estate, and unscrupulous servants take advantage of the
sheltered and uneducated girl-child who was only nineteen at her

wedding. A crisis in the marriage occurs when a chimney sweep is accidentally killed in the manor house due to the indifference of his master, Henrietta's servants, and to some extent Henrietta herself.

Adam is horrified at the child's death. He has long been aware of the abuse of child labor and is appalled to learn of what has transpired in his absence. He forces the shocked Henrietta to help him wash the child's body. Henrietta "followed the direction of his pointing finger towards the boy's groin . . . a cluster of seamed scars showed in the crotch. Adam said, in something like a recognizable voice, 'He's not only bowlegged and hunchback, he's also a eunuch. That's a scrotal infection caused by soot and known as chimney-sweep's cancer. The only treatment for it is the knife' " (*GIE*, 325). Delderfield is not loath to describe the horrors of the industrial revolution in *God Is an Englishman*.

The novel is also a business success story. Halfway through, Delderfield jumps to the late 1950s, one hundred years after the events in the novel, to show a descendant of Adam running the business in the mid–twentieth century. Algy Swann is commissioning an official one hundredth anniversary history of the firm, a clear indication that Delderfield intended to bring the story up to the 1960s. Delderfield immediately cuts back to his nineteenth-century narrative after the short, teasing contemporary interlude.

Adam has been astute in selecting his area managers, and he is a scrupulously fair and just employer, thus earning the loyalty and goodwill of his employees, which stands him in good stead when times are hard and the business has difficulties. Adam invents a calculator he calls "Frankenstein," but this helps him to plan his business and allocate human and material resources efficiently, so that after a while he is running a vast trucking, furniture removal, sight-seeing, and touring business from a yard in Bermondsey, the London locale in which, not coincidentally, Delderfield spent his early childhood.

The marriage between Henrietta and Adam, like most, has its ups and downs. After the debacle with the chimney sweep, Adam wisely forces Henrietta to become the chatelaine of the estate, and she is quick to learn to do her job well. They have a daughter and three sons in nine years. Both Adam and Henrietta are tempted at one time by the possibility of an extramarital affair. Edith Wadsworth, the lovely and efficient northern district manager, falls in love with Adam, and he is attracted to her as a modern, active, unspoiled woman. She, however, has integrity, and instead of seducing Adam helps him to strengthen his marriage. Eventually, she redeems a handsome thief and finds a good lover and husband in him. Henrietta flirts with, and is nearly raped by, a young army officer in a brilliant uniform. Both Adam and Henrietta ultimately remain faithful to each other, and the marriage not only survives all troubles but seems to thrive on them.

The great crisis is the train accident. With the help of a loyal employee, Adam rescues his family from their carriage just before it plummets over a precipice. The employee, a Hogarthian district manager named Blubb who had been a famous coachman in his youth and who hated the railway for depriving him of his original livelihood, ironically dies because a train has crashed, and his "gaffer" Adam is nearly killed by that same symbol of his competition.

Adam is in a coma. His leg is amputated. When he returns to consciousness he is shunted off to Switzerland to be fitted for an artificial limb and to learn to walk with it. Meanwhile, the business is paralyzed. Some district managers fear disintegration. Edith Wadsworth comes to the rescue and takes over the reins of the business. She goes to see Henrietta, confesses her unrequitted love for Adam, is met with friendship, and decides that the again pregnant Henrietta must be the one to lead the company so that when Adam returns he will be grateful to his wife and not to a one-time, would-be lover for saving the company—that is, if it can be saved. Henrietta is a smashing success as the "gaffer in pettycoats." She takes care of her family, runs the estate, has her healthy fourth child, and brings the business through a terrible winter by devising a system of reserve depots in the way a general on defense would establish mobile reserves to meet enemy attacks at various points. In fact, she is able to pick up excellent management skills in a matter of months, skills that it took Adam years to acquire. Her secret is that she has observed Adam's military approach to the logistics of his business, and she has extended that concept when and where it was most sorely needed.

Adam conquers his handicap and with only a slight limp returns to England after a year. He is terribly proud of Henrietta when he realizes what she has accomplished. Obviously their relationship has reached a new plane of equality, and the reader wonders how they will relate to each other when Henrietta must turn over the business to her husband. But that is a question anticipating the second volume of the Swann saga.

God Is an Englishman ends with all in order. Adam's employees surprise him with a fine gift upon his return to the yard. They have commissioned a silver sculpture of a wagon and horses, a Swann-on-Wheels vehicle. Pleased and proud, Swann thinks: "Progress was the daughter of trade, and how could the trading instinct, almost as deeply rooted in man as the sexual urge, find articulate expression without the unrestricted flow of gold and silver from one pocket to another?" (*GIE*, 686). Adam may be an enlightened employer but he is also a convinced laissez-faire capitalist.

Delderfield is more playful in *God Is an Englishman* than he is in any of his preceding novels. He enjoys the introduction of Charles Dickens, almost as a rival writer. He seems to have been rereading Shakespeare for he alludes to *Richard III*, and names several of Adam's district managers after characters in that play: Ratcliffe, Lovell, and Catesby. Also, the heroic Blubb is a Falstaffian figure who, along with Adam as a surrogate Prince Hal, thwarts a robbery à la the Gadshill episode in *Henry IV*, part one. Finally, Adam's bookkeeper is named Tybalt, from *Romeo and Juliet*.

As the touch in *God Is an Englishman* is lighter than in the earlier epics, Delderfield is not fully successful in evoking the England of industrial blight, homeless children, and expensive brothels. But character and plot excel. He has done much research into the nineteenth-century world of transportation, and it is put to excellent use in the novel. However, it is the description of domestic life in the period that is most authentic and engrossing. Furthermore, Adam as a symbol of aggressive but honorable business enterprise, and Henrietta as a symbol of the potential of Victorian womanhood, hold the reader's attention as Delderfield works his storyteller's craft with customary deftness.

Theirs Was the Kingdom. It is twelve years later in the Swann saga and the period to be covered in *Theirs Was the Kingdom* is 1878–89. If God seemed to be an Englishman to the all-conquering British of the early nineteenth century, then, with a play on "The Lord's Prayer," theirs was the kingdom of earth if not of heaven in those days of the height of empire, leading up to Queen Victoria's triumphant Golden Jubilee on 21 June 1887. Indeed, for Henrietta Swann the particular personification of the English God is Adam, her husband and her first and only man: "at morning service it was not God in His heaven she visualized but Adam Swann, riding out of the morning mists on Seddon Moor when she was a slip of a girl."[5]

Theirs Was the Kingdom is more episodal than *God Is an Englishman.* Swann-on-Wheels continues to flourish after Henrietta returned the control of the business to Adam upon the completion of his convalescence, and now, twelve years later, Adam has had twenty years in the business and Henrietta has had four more children, making a total of eight. In 1879, Mary, her last child, will be born. Josh Avery's daughter, Deborah, has been adopted by the Swanns, so all-in-all they have ten children. They are, in fact, a prototypical Victorian family. Henrietta is queen of her home and the Tryst estate, just as Victoria is the great domestic role model for the nation.

There is no great, central climax in *Theirs Was the Kingdom* comparable to the railway disaster in *God Is an Englishman*, although the book does lead up to the Golden Jubilee as Delderfield again posits a royal anniversary as a historical landmark in his fiction. On the other hand, *Theirs Was the Kingdom* is much less a panegyric to British pluck, perceptiveness, and power than is *God Is an Englishman*. It dwells more on the problems of Victorian life than the achievements, for Delderfield sharpens his critical views of British hypocrisy concerning the existence of grave social ills, especially white slavery and child prostitution. Furthermore, Delderfield assumes an even more antimilitary and anti-imperialism stance in this novel as he places the Swann's first son, Alexander, in several of Victoria's little wars and shows the clumsiness, inefficiency, stupidity, and even malfeasance of the vaunted British army.

The novel opens in December 1878 with a bird's-eye view that Delderfield often favors. The birds show the reader the Thamesside rectangle that is Swann's Bermondsey headquarters where the one-legged man with broad shoulders and friendly eyes often coaxes them with food to "the sill of the old belfry" where he keeps watch over his kingdom (*TWK*, 1). The Swann children quickly become the main focus, and it is learned that the oldest, Stella, nineteen, is already married. Unhappily, she succumbed to the temptation of a title and is trapped in a loveless, sexless relationship with a homosexual aristocrat, Lester Percy Maitland Moncton-Price, who, along with his despicable lover, Posonby, torments her. Lester's father, Sir Gilbert, who has promoted the marriage in order to obtain Swann money, now propositions Stella, hoping to use her as a breed mare to continue his line. He succeeds in getting her to strip for him, but she manages to run away without losing her virginity.

First honors in *Theirs Was the Kingdom* goes to Henrietta on the home front, for with Adam away she hides the shocked and disconsolate Stella, confronts Sir Gilbert, forces him to accept an annulment, and finally rescues her daughter from despair and life in a nunnery by relighting an old flame between Stella and a strong young farmer who has always worshiped the girl. They marry, and Stella is fecund and grows fat in her happy domestic life as the wife of an adoring farmer. She and her husband produce the first of the long line of Swann grandchildren.

Alexander, the second child, whom the romantic Henrietta had destined for the army, finds himself a boy soldier in the Zulu War, where he is one of the few British to survive the debacle of the Battle of Isandlwana (1879) in which Zulus armed with spears destroyed a British army led by an arrogant and stupid general. Delderfield is always in top form when describing military activities. Alex, fleeing for his life, "saw at a glance that it would be suicidal to attempt to ride down to river level so he threw himself out of his saddle, abandoned the horse and ran down the rocky path with men on either side of him, each jostling for elbow room, pitching, stumbling and cursing one another, and the Zulus who ran among them, lunging at any uniformed man within stabbing range. In the shallows he saw a Kaffir killed with a thrust through the throat but the man's death meant nothing to him and he splashed past the Zulu in the act of withdrawing his assegai, as though they had all been rabbiters killing for sport . . ." (*TWK*, 50).

Fortunately, Alex stumbles on to the holding action at Rorke's Drift, where in contrast to Isandlwana a relative handful of British troops, disciplined and well entrenched, hold off thousands of attacking Zulus. Ever the lucky soldier, Alex survives again and is something of a hero at eighteen, although in truth he has done little more than save his own skin. However, he sees the effects of good training, discipline, and intelligent leadership, and he decides to go to Sandhurst to learn his trade truly. As *Theirs Was the Kingdom* progresses, Alex is involved in succeeding colonial wars, is promoted when the Army in Egypt needs a hero, and eventually marries the homely but intelligent daughter of his besotted colonel. They are a perfect match. She is bright and he is brave. Lydia Corcoran Swann sees the future of the Maxim machine gun and pushes her husband into becoming the army expert on the weapon that will, of course, prove a decisive one in subsequent wars, especially in World War I, a conflict, however, that Delderfield will fail to reach in the Swann saga.

The third child, George, is the one selected by Adam to succeed him in the business, and this father-son relationship is the central parent-child development in the novel. From the beginning, and despite twists, turns, and setbacks, George represents the future of Swann-on-Wheels. Adam sends him on a tour of the company districts as soon as he finishes his schooling, and George not only learns about business but about women too. Adam then sends him to the Continent to discover developments in the transportation field there, and after romantic interludes in Paris and Munich, George makes the fateful acquaintance, in Vienna, of the old inventor and carriage builder Maximilien Körner, who is developing a prototype for a powerful horseless carriage that George sagaciously realizes is the future of the transportation business. He works with the old man on the machine, and when the senior partner has a stroke and wills him the machine before dying, George marries Körner's beautiful and devoted granddaughter Gisela and takes her and the experimental machine home to England, where he rejoins the family firm and tries to convince his father that is is time to reorganize the successful but somewhat stagnating business, to retire some of Swann's old henchmen, and to invest in the development of the horseless carriage.

Adam, however, is not only loyal to his employees to a fault, but he also sees no future in George's "toy." The two men disagree. Thanks to Henrietta's deft and wise interference, George, Gisela, their children, and the machine spirit away to Henrietta's rich old industrialist father in Manchester, Sam Rawlinson, who invests in the development of the automobile. Toward the end of the story Gisela comes to Adam and pleads with him to watch secretly the first major trials of the completed prototype truck. He does so and he quickly realizes:. "God help me, I've been wrong all the time! His vehicle was carrying freight and nothing I possess in the way of wagons and teams could cover the ground at half the speed" (*TWK*, 761).

Adam and George reconcile on the spot. The older man, now sixty-two, gets his first ride in an automobile and immediately decides that George must take over the firm. The age of mechanization is upon them, and George is the businessman Swann prepared for it, as Alex is the warrior Swann also prepared for the new age with his faith in the machine gun.

The fourth Swann child, Giles, a young man of a sensitive, poetic nature, is also of importance in *Theirs Was the Kingdom*. Delderfield sends Giles to good old West Buckland School where he receives an excellent post-Arnoldian education. The boy turns down a chance to go to Oxford in order to make a walking tour of the country, where he is sensitized to the terrible working conditions of the Welsh miners and the Lancashire mill workers. He realizes that his father's Gladstonian position and respect for his two thousand employees is the best path for industrial Britain.

On his trek Giles meets Romayne Rycroft-Mostyn, the beautiful, impish, spoiled daughter of one of Britain's wealthiest industrialists. Although they are both only eighteen, they fall madly in love and pledge their troth. Both families are pleased, but the courtship and the wait for majority is rocky because of Romayne's immaturity and insensitivity. When she displays gross selfishness and callousness toward working-class girls, Giles sadly breaks off the engagement although he still loves her deeply. Romayne is heartbroken and disappears. Giles accidently finds her over a year later. She has been doing a self-imposed penance, working anonymously in a retail shop under terrible conditions. She is wane and broken, and Giles's heart goes out to her again. They quickly marry, and Giles, refusing to work for his rich but exploitive father-in-law, goes into Swann-on-Wheels as director of employee benefits and pensions.

None of the other of the nine biological Swann children figure significantly in the story to date, although they have their adventures too, and Henrietta must produce and direct a mock elopement for pregnant daughter Joanna. However, the adopted child, Deborah Avery, who is, in fact, five years older than Stella, is as important to the family history as any of the other children, with the exception of George, for it is Deborah, even more than Giles, who is the family conscience and consciousness raiser. She has been well educated and has devoted her life to reform, serving with the crusading editor W. T. Stead in the war against British Victorian hypocrisy concerning white slavery and prostitution. She is savagely whipped in an amateurish attempt to expose a white slave ring kidnapping and despoiling British girls in Brussels, thus provoking her mysterious biological father, Josh Avery, to come out of hiding for a brief moment and to take revenge for her by obtaining the evidence she risked her life to get. He also pays back Adam all the company money he had squandered on his Spanish lover years before, and then he disappears again.

Deborah and Stead, a real-life crusading journalist who went to prison for his principles and who later drowned on the *Titantic*, appeal to the great decency in Adam, and he takes a courageous stand against child prostitution, the first important English businessman to do so. Delderfield then belatedly gives Deborah a love interest and, although past thirty, like a good Delderfield heroine she marries and accepts "natural" domesticity.

As *Theirs Was the Kingdom* ends, Henrietta has reached menopause, but she and Adam continue to enjoy frequent, lusty sex. He packs up his trophies and mementos in London and moves them to Tryst. There he plans a transportation museum where "anyone who wanted to trace the history of the enterprise, when he was safely tucked away in Twyforde Green churchyard . . . could come and potter among the flotsam of his youth" (*TWK*, 776), including his calculator-computer invention, Frankenstein. Also, Adam, still a youthful sixty-three, sets out to turn Tryst into a country showplace of good taste.

Adam's business career has been a great success due in large part to his unwavering, ethical approach. He has always known that "pinchpenny wages and brutish conditions defeat their own objects." It should not be capital versus labor: "Call it Capital-*plus*-Labour and get ahead as a team!" (*TWK*, 123).

Henrietta has evolved into an outstanding parent, wife, helpmate, and estate manager. It seems as if her development has forced the author to reassess his view of the strengths, capabilities, dreams, and desires of women in general, for again and again in *Theirs Was the Kingdom* women—like George's various lovers; his wife, Gisela; Stella with her husband Denzil; Alex's wife, Lydia; and Deborah with her husband, Milton—take the lead in matters sexual and social, professional as well as domestic.

Now Adam's business career is over, and the firm is in George's competent hands. The apogee of the British Empire and an English family have been reached. It is time for Adam and Henrietta to observe and no longer to actuate. Their twilight world is destined, however, to grow darker and more difficult.

Parts of *Theirs Was the Kingdom* are repetitious. Too often

Delderfield reiterates past events, particularly from *God Is an English-man*, partly because the story is so long and there are so many threads to it that he feels it necessary to refresh reader memory frequently, and partly because he wishes the novel to stand on its own legs. This it does not do. It is a bridge, and it neither climaxes nor concludes despite the fact that the reader is firmly held in the fictional web, still eager for installments of the Swann saga.

Give Us This Day. It is the old age of Adam and Henrietta Swann, and Adam at least is quite glad for each new day God gives him as he comes to realize: "I've had a wonderful innings and ought not to resent making way for others. If only they'll learn to value it—this corner of an old landscape, and the way of life that goes with it. . . ."[6] The Lord's Prayer is fully answered for this good couple; they have over fifty years together.

Give Us This Day begins eight years after *Theirs Was the Kingdom* and covers the period from June 1897, the month of the celebration of Queen Victoria's Diamond Jubilee and Adam's seventieth birthday, to July 1914, a seventeen-year period. The family, in various places and ways, celebrates the Jubilee. Henrietta's father, eighty-eight-year-old Sam Rawlinson, dies shortly after the story reopens, just as Adam's father, Colonel Swann, died at the beginning of *Theirs Was the Kingdom.*

Adam has remained in retirement, a laconic landscaper and connoisseur, obsessed with his estate and still enjoying sex with his bosomy wife. But there is trouble in Swann lake. George, in charge of Swann-on-Wheels, has not succeeded in introducing motorized vans in to the business because his machines proved unreliable. Horse and wagon seem destined to ride on forever. Disappointed and bored, George at thirty-three has been seduced into a love affair with a rich, married woman and has neglected the business, allowing a dishonest head accountant to rob the firm. Adam gets wind of trouble and sets out to investigate just as Henrietta begins to read Sherlock Holmes. The business is nearly totally destroyed as the thief sets fire to the headquarters yard to cover his tracks. Adam, ever strong and re-sourceful, steps back into the business to rebuild it and allows George a year away in Manchester to perfect mechanical transport and rebuild his marriage, both of which he does.

George's story is the main of many threads in *Give Us This Day* as he slowly grows into the patriarch figure, supplants Adam as the rock of the family, comes to the rescue of various family members, and,

after initial rejection by the Swann board of directors, brings about
the complete mechanization of the company, when, in the central
incident of the book, he miraculously transports a six-ton naval gun
turret across the entire country using trucks in tandem.

Alexander, the family professional soldier, is no Alexander the
Great, but a somewhat stodgy, snobbish, plodding soldier fighting
his hide-bound, term-serving superiors more than the queen's enemies as he struggles to modernize the army. He rises to rank of
lieutenant colonel but plays a small part in this novel, serving
primarily as a foil to Giles, who evolves from a parlor radical to a
Liberal anti–Boer War politician, friend and supporter of Lloyd
George, and member of Parliament. Alexander's and Giles's differing
views of the justness of the Boer War create a deep schism in the
family. Still, Alex remains Henrietta's favorite child, "the only one
among them who fulfilled her girlish dream of mothering a race of
scarlet-clad warriors . . . " (*GUTD*, 367).

Giles's wife, Romayne, now ever supportive of her husband's career, begins to provide him with children after thirteen years of
marriage, and then, with his encouragement, becomes a follower of
Mrs. Emmeline Pankhurst, the leader of the militant Women's Social
and Political Union. Jailed many times and tortured for her views,
Romayne, who develops into a character not dissimilar from Grace in
A Horseman Riding By, is run over and killed in a Suffragist demon-
stration. Giles suffers terribly but eventually finds love and happiness
again. In a passage clearly foreshadowing the next volume of the
Swann saga, never written of course, Adam believes "that it was
Giles and his successors who would live here (Tryst) some day when
he was dust and maybe some of them would come to think of it as he
was beginning to think of it, the only worthwhile legacy one generation could pass to another. Land and what grew on it" (*GUTD*, 236).

The fourth son, Hugo, barely mentioned in *Theirs Was the Kingdom*, is quite important in *Give Us This Day*. The dull athlete,
winner of countless running trophies, develops into a war hero and
almost saintlike healer due in no small part to the ambition and then
the love of the forceful woman who captures him, Lady Sybil, eldest
daughter of the earl of Uskdale.

Sybil falls in lust with Hugo's beautiful body at a track meet. She
courts and wins the diffident and unsophisticated young man and
then sets out to turn him into a proper husband for an influential
aristocratic bluestocking. Unfortunately, her program includes ob-

taining Hugo a commission in the army in the Boer War (1899–1902), a badly handled Vietnam-like affair for the British. Completely untrained, he is useless in battle until he has a chance to sprint through Boer fire to locate a relief party. He succeeds, but is shot through the head and blinded for life when he doubles back to offer covering fire for his trapped comrades. His last sight is that of the face of an enemy boy soldier he shot, and that vision haunts him throughout his life.

Appalled by what her machinations have done to simple, decent Hugo, Sybil dedicates her life to making it up to him. She helps him to find an independent life and career as a protophysical therapist in veterans' hospitals where his strength, courage, fame, and optimism inspire his fellow wounded and maimed so that he becomes a living legend and is knighted. Adam best understands Hugo's contribution, saying: "Go down to Netley and watch him at work on patients. I did that . . . and came away humbled. I'm not a religious man but I believe in some miracles. One has to when one hears a blind man preach a sermon through his fingertips" (*GUTD*, 541).

The Hugo plot allows Delderfield the opportunity to exercise his great ability at describing public events such as athletic meets, parliamentary debates, political rallies, demonstrations, public funerals, and of course battle scenes. As Hugo's cavalry unit is being routed, Delderfield paints the scene: "Dead and dying troopers were everywhere among terrified horses, some of them hit and screaming with pain. Dust rose in a red cloud, obliterating the field of fire. Equipment, including a scatter of long, useless lances, lay everywhere. A sergeant sat with his back to a rock, trying to staunch a spouting wound in his thigh and blood spattered Hugo as he stepped over his legs, making for a knot of unwounded men cowering behind a larger rock and emptying their magazines at nothing" (*GUTD*, 239).

The daughters Joanna and Helen make interesting contributions to the story. In *Theirs Was the Kingdom* the pregnant Joanna eloped with happy-go-lucky Clinton Coles. They now live in Dublin where Clinton is a Swann district head and where they are happy despite the fact that he runs around a little and drinks a lot. Helen has married Clinton's brother Roland, who has become a missionary doctor in China. She hates the hard life and her ascetic husband's lack of sexual interest. They are caught up in the Boxer Rebellion (1899–1900), and Roland, trying to give medical aid to the Chinese, is beheaded.

His severed head is delivered to Helen. The shocked woman takes refuge along with hundreds of other Europeans in the international compound in Peking where they are besieged for seven weeks until rescued by European and Japanese troops. Atavistically, Helen's soldiering Swann blood rises and she takes revenge for Roland, shooting to death a Chinese officer at the barricades.

Home at Tryst Helen is wasting away when, in the most bizarre episode in the Swann saga, Joanna, ever loving and close to her sister, "lends" Helen her drunk husband for a night to stop her bad dreams. Clinton never realizes that there has been a substitution. It is the old bed trick from classical and Renaissance literature. Furthermore, Delderfield would have the reader believe that a few seconds of a drunken man's thrusting could cure a woman, deprived of sex for a year, of depression and most anything else that ails her.

Joanna takes Helen back to Dublin, where the widow meets and wins the heart of the city's most eligible bachelor, Rory Clarke, an Irish patriot and a founder of the militant Sinn Fein. The couple become caught up in the Irish struggle for independence. One of the discordant notes at the end of the novel is that Rory is planning armed rebellion and collaboration with the Germans in 1914.

Another discordant note is the suffering of the oldest Swann child, Stella, the matronly wife of the farmer Denzil Fawcett. They have had six children. Two of their sons have left the farm to work in the automotive trades for George. Martin, the brightest one, is accidentally killed test driving George's business-saving invention, the articulated lorry, the modern tractor trailer. Stella's sorrow, pain, and anger drive her out of her mind and she first tries to shoot George and then drowns herself in a nearby stream, a fat, middle-aged, sad caricature of Ophelia, seemingly meeting the destiny she had avoided over thirty years before when she escaped her homosexual husband and his rapacious father.

The last two Swann children play minor roles in *Give Us This Day*. Edward is a chip off the old block, a valuable member of the Swann company, who, unfortunately, marries the stunningly beautiful Gilda Wickstead, the cold-hearted daughter of Edith Wadsworth Wickstead, Adam's old friend. After only a few months of icy marriage, she deserts the heartbroken Edward and runs away to become, eventually, a Hollywood movie star. Edith, however, has a replacement in store for Edward in the form of her lusty, good-natured, hoydenish niece, Betsy, who resuscitates Edward with large doses of good sex.

Again in *Give Us This Day*, Delderfield's women, for the most part, are the sexually aggressive partners.

Margaret, the youngest Swann, is a quiet, attractive woman, a painter like her paternal grandfather, the old colonel. To Henrietta's chagrin, she falls in love with and marries Huw Griffiths, a strong, handsome Welsh coal miner. However, it is a happy marriage.

The novel progresses majestically from one historical or family anniversary to another: the Diamond Jubilee of Victoria; her great funeral in 1901, which Adam attends and describes like a news commentator; the Swann Golden Jubilee banquet in 1908 marking the firm's fiftieth anniversary; the funeral of Edward VII, the old peacemaker, the man who gladly made love, not war; and the great national debate leading to the entry of Great Britain into World War I, just as the novel closes. Through all the change and trauma Swann's way persists: live life with gusto, God's design is there and will disclose itself, do the best one can "without treading the next man underfoot" (*GUTD*, 767). It that way, Delderfield implies, good guys finish first.

As the novel ends Adam is eighty-seven. He has had remarkably good health during a very long life despite being wounded in action in youth and deprived of a leg near the age of forty. Again Delderfield has his hero come to the end of a rich life, full of eventful years, with strength and dignity. The Paul Craddocks and Adam Swanns of Delderfield's fiction never grow senile, never have debilitating diseases. They remain strong, dignified, clear-headed, and ready to the end to stiffen up their progeny with advice or action. Both heroes and heroines achieve old age as writer and reader would like it to be, not as it always is.

However, it must be pointed out that Adam technically does not die as *Give Us This Day* ends. "He closed his eyes" (*GUTD*, 767). Delderfield may have intended to restate his death and describe his funeral in the next volume. Alas, it was the stopping of the novel machine that ended the Swann saga.

Give Us This Day has the most fragmented structure of the three Swann books, resulting naturally from the fanning out of the Swann children, grandchildren, and great grandchildren, who are hatched in swarms. The business and technical descriptions grow somewhat esoteric, and the social and political history are laid on with a heavier trowel than in the two earlier novels. As the saga progresses it seems less influenced by the Forsyte chronicles than by Anthony Trollope's

six political novels on the dynastic marriage of the politician Plantagenet Palliser and Lady Glencora, and the lives of their children,
which in fact cover some of the same period and historical events as
does the Swann saga. If Delderfield had lived longer, the Swann saga
might have grown to be as long as the Palliser story. As it stands, it
is a monumental epic of the growth of British trade and industry
with a hero of noble stature who is a businessman.

Chapter Eight
Miscellany

That R. F. Delderfield was a prolific writer—one who published millions of words of fiction and drama in his lifetime—is obvious both to scholars of twentieth-century British literature and to his many readers. That his work encompassed other genres besides the novel and the drama is less well known. His narrative skills were simply unlimited. They were hardly even controllable, and they found outlets everywhere, especially in history and autobiography, but also in travel writing and writing for young people.

History

In the field of history R. F. Delderfield achieved a minor reputation among professional historians as an expert on Napoleon. From youth Delderfield was fascinated by the life and the times of the great Frenchman who gave his name to an age and his dream of a united Europe to the future. Delderfield put his scholar's knowledge of the Napoleonic period to excellent use in two novels discussed above: *Seven Men of Gascony* and *Too Few for Drums*. Additionally, *Farewell, the Tranquil Mind* treats the period of Revolutionary French history immediately preceding the rise to power of the young Corsican artillery captain.

Delderfield wrote five Napoleonic histories: *Napoleon in Love* (1959), *The March of the Twenty-Six: The Story of Napoleon's Marshals* (1962), *The Golden Millstones: Napoleon's Brothers and Sisters* (1964), *The Retreat from Moscow* (1967), and *Imperial Sunset: The Fall of Napoleon 1813–1814* (1969). In so doing, and by dealing with, in rippling circles of affection and connection, his wives and lovers, his relatives, his marshals, and the Grand Army, Delderfield consciously or unconsciously created a biography by circumscription. The portrait of Napoleon he painted was that of a driven man of astounding energy, immense shrewdness, the very Mars of his time, yet a man loyal to a fault when it came to loved ones, family, and comrades-in-arms, always remaining, to paraphrase Shakespeare's *Richard II*, a man who lived by bread, felt want, needed friends. Delderfield's Napoleon is both a complex genius and an incurable romantic.

Delderfield's skill and contribution as an historian is not in the realm of revisionism or reinterpretation. He is a gatherer, evaluator, and analyzer of primary documents and secondary sources that he synthesizes and then brilliantly illuminates by means of his ability to delineate character, to narrate events so that they become three-dimensional, and to re-create a milieu in the minds of his readers. During most of the years Delderfield was a novelist, he was a working historian as well.

Napoleon in Love. *Napoleon in Love* is the tastefully told story of the great emperor's quest for romantic fulfillment. He had two wives and a dozen serious mistresses. In the twenty-five years from his marriage to Joséphine Beauharnais to his death in exile on the rock of St. Helena, "he made love to at least fourteen women: all were young, attractive and extremely eager to please."[1] Delderfield does not condemn Napoleon's infidelity and promiscuousness. Instead, he points out that neither aristocrats nor politicians then "regarded the married state as a barrier to the enjoyment of mistresses" (*NIL*, 13). Delderfield states that although Napoleon's many conquests in the field of love are as impressive as his many victories in the field of battle, and there is no Waterloo among them, there is a curious "sterility" and sense of shallowness about them. In his favor Napoleon loved women, had great sexual vigor, and to the very end of his life his attitude toward the opposite sex was, "in the main, as

uncomplicated as that of a schoolboy and often as nearly as tender" (*NIL*, 12).

Delderfield concentrates on Napoleon's relationship with his wives, the greedy, unfaithful, Empress Joséphine, and the vacuous, overly protected Empress Marie Louise, who married the forty-year-old campaigner when she was eighteen, and of whom Delderfield says, "There never was a bride who went more innocently to her marriage bed" (*NIL*, 204), but who was able to give her husband what her predecessor could not: a son, Napoleon II, the king of Rome, who grew to manhood and died without ever ruling a single Frenchman or Italian or anyone else for that matter.

Napoleon in Love also features the major supporting cast of Napoleon's lovers, but the most moving story concerns the relationship between the emperor and the beautiful Polish countess, Marie Walewska, who was pushed into his bed in order to help Poland to independence and who grew to love the emperor as no other woman ever did. The study is not a series of episodes in a bedroom farce, but an illumination of the intimate side of the character of a shaker of nations and how that aspect of character helped shape his career and the destiny of Europe.

Light and popular history though it may be, *Napoleon in Love* leaves the reader with the kind of valid insights into a great person's mind, heart, and spirit that many, more scholarly books do not begin to offer.

The March of the Twenty-Six: The Story of Napoleon's Marshals. Between the years 1804, when he took the crown as emperor, and the year 1815, when he suffered his final defeat at Waterloo, Napoleon created twenty-six marshals of France. These men, who held great power, came from diverse backgrounds, for their chief often proclaimed that a marshal's baton was concealed in the knapsack of every private soldier in the armies of France. It was superb motivation and great propaganda. These enterprising soldiers grasped at crowns, quarreled, intrigued, marched, fought, suffered, and died for a soldier who was more loyal to them than they were to him.

Kellerman, Sérurier, and Davout began as junior officers in the army. Murat was an innkeeper's son who became the king of Naples. Lefèbvre was a hussar, Pérignon a grenadier, and Marmont an artilleryman. Moncey started as a lawyer, Jourdan a peddlar, Masséna a cabin boy, and Augereau a footman. Bernadotte was an ex-sergeant major who became king of Sweden. Victor had been a sergeant too. Soult had wanted to be a baker, Brune a writer, and Oudinot a brewer. Macdonald was the son of an exiled Scot. Poniatowski was the nephew of a Polish prince and was born to the soldier's trade, and Grouchy also was the son of an aristocrat. Ney was a cooper, Lannes a dyer, Mortier a farmer, and St. Cyr and Berthier were engineers. Bessières was a barber at first, and Suchet came from a family of silk manufacturers. Delderfield shows how their personalities and ambitions affected the events of the Napoleonic era. Thus *The March of the Twenty-Six* is essentially an interweaving of concise biographies in front of a panorama of battles, conquests, victories, defeats, and routs.

The two most interesting lives in the book are those of Alexandre Berthier, Napoleon's chief of staff and master planner who, when the battle was joined, would put down his pen and rush to the sound of the guns, where "sabre in hand he jostled others "to be first through a curtain of fire";[2] and the greatest French general of the time, next to Napoleon, Michel Ney, who brought the rear guard out of Russia, and who had so much charisma that when he ordered his trapped and frostbitten troops to retreat eastward toward the enemy and they protested his outrageous but wise order, he said: "Very well, I'll go to Smolensk alone!" (*NM*, 196). They followed and they lived.

The March of the Twenty-Six is stirring biographical history. It exudes panache. Delderfield's admiration for these men is almost unlimited. Most important, however, he indicates that the greatest resource Napoleon had was twenty-six superb generals. In a sense, compositely, they *were* Napoleon.

The Golden Millstones: Napoleon's Brothers and Sisters. "I do not believe that any man in the world is more unfortunate in his family than I am!," Napoleon said in 1810 at the height of his power.[3] He was right; the family was an expensive luxury to him. His brothers and sisters, "their marriages, their progeny, their extravagance, quarrels and ceaseless intrigues continued to harass the man who never could rid himself of the responsibilities he had assumed when Carlo Buonaparte (his father) had died more than twenty years before" (*GM*, 151). Delderfield shows, however, that Napoleon's troubles with his siblings were to a large extent of his own making as he continually tried to control their lives and use them for his dynastic purposes. Thus *The Golden Millstones*, meaning of course his brothers and sisters, is the story of the rise and fall of a family.

Delderfield uses the same format in *The Golden Millstones* that he employed in *The March of the Twenty-Six*: interweaving biographies, in this case several parallel stories over a period of sixty years. However, this effort is not as successful as *The March of the Twenty-Six*, for its narrative is somewhat jerky and the author relies on gossip and innuendo to a considerably greater extent than even in *Napoleon in Love*. Nevertheless, that gang of seven were a fascinating accumulation of greed, venality, vanity, ambition, immorality, stubbornness, and ingratitude, and the author nearly succeeds in bringing them to life again.

The oldest of the Buonaparte children was Joseph, who became king of Naples and then king of Spain but never possessed any real power and only wanted to live a quiet rural life. After Waterloo he emigrated to America and spent many happy years in New Jersey and refused the throne of Mexico. Napoleon was the second child. The third was Lucien, the only sibling to defy his brother's wishes and get away with it. He rejected a throne because he did not wish to give up his second wife for a dynastic marriage. Captured by the British, he learned to live as an English country gentleman. As a young man, however he saved Napoleon from near political failure and probable death through his great oratorical skill.

Elisa, the fourth child, married a lumbering major of infantry and begged for a title. Napoleon made her a duchess. Louis, the next child, shared Napoleon's early barracks days and then saved his brother's life in an early battle. Napoleon made him king of Holland but he had an unhappy marriage, often vexed his brother, and suffered from debilitating syphilis. Long before the First Empire collapsed he abdicated his responsibilities and retired to a private life.

Pauline was a "pleasure-loving harlot" (*GM*, 194), called by competent judges the greatest beauty of the age. She wedded a general, and after his death she married the greatest practical joker in Europe. Always promiscuous, she posed naked to the waist for Canova, the Venetian sculptor. Napoleon was always indulgent to his beautiful sister. In the end she alone shared his exile in Elba and then tried to join him on St. Helena. Caroline was also a great beauty. She married Napoleon's wild cavalry marshal, Murat, and became queen of Naples, but turned traitor to her brother.

Jérôme was the most prodigal of the family. He failed as a sailor,

he failed as a soldier, and he failed as king of Westphalia. On a visit
to America when a youth he met and married an American girl, then
deserted her at Napoleon's insistence. He married twice more. Joseph
had one moment of valor at Waterloo and he survived to a revered
and prosperous old age.

Delderfield claimed that his interest in the Napoleonic period
began "when he gazed at Napoleon's coach in Madame Tussaud's at
the age of six and went home with a curiosity about him that lasted
a lifetime" (*GM*, 238). In *Napoleon in Love*, *The March of the Twenty-
Six*, and *The Golden Millstones*, Delderfield satiated that curiosity and
fulfilled a need to share with his reading public both his knowledge
of and fascination for the man who kept all Europe in a boiling
cauldron for nineteen years. Delderfield's last two histories, then,
dealt with campaigns, and the author chose to write about later ones,
Russia and the last stand before Elba.

The Retreat from Moscow.   Like most historians of the First
Empire Delderfield was perplexed and fascinated by Napoleon's
greatest blunder, one which Charles XII of Sweden had committed
before him in the time of Peter the Great and which Hitler committed in the twentieth century. Since he could not occupy so vast a
country, why did Europe's greatest strategist undertake such a huge,
punitive expedition against Czar Alexander II when he had so much
to lose and so little to gain? If he wished to secure the Eastern border
of a Europe united under his eagle, why did he not stop at the
Russian border after he had "liberated" the duchy of Warsaw? The
grateful Poles would have been his vassals for a generation at least.
These are some of the historical questions Delderfield raises and
discusses in *The Retreat from Moscow*, his excitingly and vividly presented version of the Grand Army's immolation in the time from 24
June 1812 when "the largest force ever assembled in modern times,"[4]
the undefeated hammer of Napoleon, crossed the Niemen and took
"the greatest gamble of modern history up to that time" (*RFM*, 15),
until Marshal Ney, France's most valiant general officer, staggered
backwards across the Niemen's bridge, the last man of the rear
guard, still defiantly facing the ever-pursuing Cossacks, only 179
days later. Left behind was the near total wreckage of an army of
350,000, a ruined countryside, a devastated Moscow, and the future
of the French Empire. Delderfield points out that "In terms of military achievement even the Nazi invasions of 1941 were more positive
than that" (*RFM*, 15).

Retreat from Moscow is penned with skill in depicting the characters and personalities of the tragic campaign. The cast of characters from *The March of the Twenty-Six* take the stage again in this work as they also do subsequently in *Imperial Sunset*. To create this verbal panorama Delderfield draws on eyewitness narratives from their period and, as in the past, successfully weaves them together to create an appealing and breathtaking story.

Imperial Sunset: The Fall of Napoleon, 1813–1814. The period covered in *Imperial Sunset* is that immediately following the retreat from Russia and preceding the first exile to Elba and the return to power in the one hundred days before Waterloo. It is a period between two great and tragic cataclysms, the defeat in Russia and the end at Waterloo, and thus often neglected by historians. It should not be. As Delderfield points out, in the sixteen months immediately following the abandonment of Moscow Napoleon fought a brilliant military and political campaign to achieve a peace that might keep him on the throne of France. But it was the autumn of his empire, the cavalry had been depleted in Russia, and there was no way to exploit battlefield victories. Most important of all, the Allies finally had learned not to sue for peace individually after a single defeat, but to accept their losses, regroup, and hang in the campaign. Finally, Napoleon was decisively defeated at Leipzig. He had to retreat across the Rhine minus two thirds of his army, and the Allies poured into France forcing the emperor's abdication and the restoration of the Bourbons to the throne. The Allies now could also restore privilege and extirpate the dangerous policy of meritocracy that had been the major political and psychological innovation behind Napoleon's rise to power and his control over the army and the people.

In the end Napoleon surrendered to the Royal Navy to save his life. A British tar offered a valediction: "Good health, Your Honor, and better luck next time."[5] But it was not really all over yet. "From all parts of Europe, as summer succeeded spring, long files of footsore men in patched, threadbare uniforms, trudged towards the frontiers of France. They were prisoners of war, released under the terms of peace, begging their way home to the land they had left as seasoned fighters or conscripts in the string of campaigns that had convulsed the Continent in an almost unbroken succession of wars" (*IS*, 286). Shortly, these men would form the new army of the one hundred glorious and tragic days that led from Elba to Waterloo to St. Helena and the end of the dream of a united Europe. Delderfield has some of the returning war prisoners trudging past the hamlet of Waterloo where many of them would soon die. The book's last word is "Waterloo." It is as if Delderfield was thinking of a sixth Napoleonic history, one on the Waterloo campaign, but one he would never write.

In *The Fall of Napoleon* Delderfield, by now an absolute master of historical narrative, handles his complicated military, political, and social material with deftness. Here again, the author exposes his bias toward the French in that long trial by combat called the Napoleonic Wars, and there is a touch of nostalgia in the writing as well as a longing for a Europe that could have avoided the cataclysms of the next century, known as World War I, World War II, and the cold war had it been united and federalized in 1812.

The writing of popular history, Delderfield's kind, is undoubtedly a useful activity, as he well realized. It gives the layman and the beginning historian insights into the past that help them to understand the present and contemplate the future. The gleaning and embellishment of source documents and memoirs is a craft in itself. Delderfield was a master of that one too.

Autobiography

R. F. Delderfield wrote four autobiographical studies, two in the early 1950s and two in the late 1960s, close to the end of his life: *Nobody Shouted Author* (1951), *Bird's Eye View: An Autobiography* (1954), *For My Own Amusement* (1968), and *Overture for Beginners* (1970). In toto they present the image of a man who loves life and his family; is cynical about theater, writers, and artists in general; cares for his country but not for its governments; is amused by, but longs for the acceptance of, the natives of his adopted Devon; and is not much concerned with spiritual or metaphysical questions. Delderfield makes no claim for himself as a major writer or as a theorist of the novel. He expresses content with his ability in the craft of storytelling.

Nobody Shouted Author. In thirty-one short pieces Delderfield essays such diverse topics as his London childhood, his aunts and uncles, his marriage to May, their first homes, an abortive attempt at chicken and egg farming, amateur theater in Britain, his continuing love for Hollywood films, and, most interestingly, his experiences and views concerning the London stage in the 1940s. In the title essay Delderfield satirizes his experience in professional theater production. In it he gently attacks actors, producers, the critics, and the audience, who drown out his dialogue with "the rustle of programmes, the isolated clang of a late . . . arrival's seat, and the hacking cough of the inevitable thirty-one consumptives in the dress circle . . ."(*NSA*, 143).

Bird's Eye View. Delderfield's second autobiography is much more formal. There he writes of his life from his birth in 1912 to his achieving fame as a dramatist in the early 1950s. His structural technique is to divide his life into two to six-year segments and focus on specific events or experiences that either climaxed or typified the period. These include his childhood terrors during World War I zeppelin raids; his move with his family to the suburbs in 1918; early schooling; the exodus to Devon, where the female sex enters his life and where he learned that he "wanted to sample kissing" and "found it wholly delightful" (*BEV*, 62–63); his favorite teachers, newspaper experience, beginning play writing, courtship and marriage, military life, and reaching the West End.

A particularly significant revelation in *Bird's Eye View* is how very distant Delderfield's early life and training were from the world of theater and belles lettres. His success came from extremely hard work, sustained self-teaching and observation, and perseverance, as well as, of course, innate talent.

For My Own Amusement. Writing some fourteen years after *Bird's Eye View*, Delderfield chose in *For My Own Amusement* to go over much of the same ground he covered in the earlier work. This time, however, he is writing as an internationally renown novelist instead of a recently successful playwright. Thus Delderfield shifts the autobiographical emphasis toward delineating sources in his own experience for characters and events in his fiction. He speaks of his disillusionment with the stage; the changing fashions, styles, and values during the evolving decades of his life; and, most significantly, he paints deft portraits of friends and acquaintances who clearly served as models for key characters in his work. Furthermore, this optimistic man refuses to put down modern youth. If they have a characteristic that differentiates them from their parent's generation, it is that they take themselves and their lives too seriously. For his own generation, those who endured and survived two world wars, the

Great Depression, and the bubbling cauldron of East-West tension, he concludes: "We worked and played harder and we certainly laughed and dreamed a lot more" (*FMOA*, 1968, 11).

The American edition of *For My Own Amusement*, published in 1972, differs from the British edition. It does not have six of the pieces originally published, and it contains two pieces not included in the original. The effect, an essay in nostalgic reminiscence, endures, however.

Overture for Beginners. *Overture for Beginners* looks again at people, places, events, and experiences covered in both *Bird's Eye View* and *For My Own Amusement*, this time with the emphasis on his familial relationships, his courting of May, and his life in the 1920s and 1930s. He pays a special, loving tribute to his older brother William, with whom he was reunited after a thirty-five-year interval. William, who had been living in Australia, returned to visit England shortly after their father's death, and the reunion startled Delderfield with the "impression that my father had recrossed the Jordan radiating a rare tolerance acquired during his brief sojourn among the Blessed"(*OFB*, 43).

Overture for Beginners adds little to what can be learned about the author's life and thought in the earlier autobiographies, but it does succeed in projecting his geniality, his self-effacing humor, and his sharp powers of observation and recall. The biographical works of R. F. Delderfield are charming readings in themselves. Like the sagas, they evoke time and place with clarity and precision. They also serve as keys to the sources of the raw materials of characters, incidents, locales, and attitudes presented in Delderfield's fiction and drama.

Travel

In 1962 and 1963 Delderfield made three automobile tours, driving some three thousand miles within England while avoiding London and the home counties.[6] He began each journey in Exeter and first drove to York and back, then to Scotland and back, and finally to Land's End and return. He drove slowly and stopped frequently on his Mr. Sermon—like solitary adventure. The first result was that Delderfield learned much about his fellow English and the lives that they led, particularly in the small towns, villages, and rural areas. The second result was that he gathered much local color and material for what would become the Swann saga. Lastly, he wrote a charming travel book, *Under an English Sky*, which depicts his journey in precise and loving detail. The book stands as an excellent mid-century description of English life yet untouched by the demographic and economic changes that had affected London and the other larger urban centers. One of his many discoveries on his sentimental journey is why the English wait in line so patiently: "The English queue patiently because a queue is a compromise between bureaucracy and a free-for-all, both of which the English distrust."[7]

For Youth

The Adventures of Ben Gunn is a gift to young people and a homage to Delderfield's favorite childhood author, Robert Louis Stevenson, and the book Delderfield read "at least once a year" since he was thirteen: *Treasure Island.*[8] It is dedicated to his children, Veronica and Paul, and it stemmed from questions they asked their father when he read *Treasure Island* to them, such as "What *made* a promising man like Silver bad in the first place?" and "How did a dear harmless creature like Ben Gunn become a pirate in the first place" (*BG*, 10). *The Adventures of Ben Gunn* is essentially an answer to the latter, a "pre-quel" to the Stevenson classic.

Stevenson's hero, Jim Hawkins, is living a squire's life in Devon, a neighbor to the old, reformed pirate, Ben Gunn, who before his death gave Jim permission to write down the story of his life. The novel is thus Jim's account of Ben's miserable childhood; his running away to sea with his master, Nick Allardyce; his meeting Hands, Pew, Flint, Bones, and Long John Silver; and his joining the pirate band that eventually marooned him on Kidd's Island. *The Adventures of Ben Gunn* is a good idea. The plot is almost as busy and exciting as Stevenson's. As is correct in writing for youth, Delderfield presents a strong and clear case for Ben's basic worth as a person. His society offered him little in the way of opportunity, it impressed its seamen, it transported poachers, and it punished minor offenses draconically, thus provoking defensive counterattacks by the victimized: counterattacks that created desperadoes. Delderfield also succeeds in capturing much of Stevenson's style and atmosphere so that his book dovetails well with that of his childhood idol. In the end the enigmatic Long John Silver, the true-hero villain of both works, remains at liberty, and, who knows, may yet be "singing and shouting about [his] trade among the islands of the Golden West" (*BG*, 222).

Chapter Nine
Achievement and Summation

The author R. F. Delderfield began his writing career on the outer fringes of the belletristic world: a journalist on a provincial weekly owned by his father. He wrote plays for amateur societies like the one in his town of Exmouth because he thought he could write them as well or better than those turning them out. The trauma, disruption, danger, and boredom of duty in the R.A.F. in World War II served as a catalyst for Delderfield, and the unexpected success of his early play, *Worm's Eye View*, established him as a leading playwright in the commercial West End theater. But he never had a second success approaching the extraordinary long run of his first London hit.

Slowly, R. F. Delderfield came to realize that his talent lay as a storyteller and that his natural subject was the life of his fellow Britons in the years he knew well, the first three quarters of the twentieth century, in the places he knew best, inner London, the suburbs, and the West Country of Devon. His scope and vision continually extended as he grew as an artist so that his subjects and themes required three-decker treatment and even longer formats if he had been given more time. He traveled little. He never hob-nobbed with the literati. He was very happy in his adopted Devon. He settled into the spacious rooms of his imagination. His work become his life, so that mere single-volume novels and histories become relaxing interludes in his re-creation of late nineteenth- and twentieth-century British life. In the end and summarily, R. F. Delderfield left for posterity exactly what he wanted to leave: a vast panorama of Britain, particularly England, depicting that nation's trials and tribulations from the early industrial revolution through the colonial wars of the nineteenth century, the humiliation of the Boer War, the growth of socialism in Britain, the great cataclysms of World War I, the depression, World War II, and the end of the empire. His vivid, broadly stroked characters are witnesses to what a future Gibbons will call the decline and fall of the British Empire. Delderfield is twentieth-century Britain's prose Homer and his sagas are its *Iliad* and *Odyssey*. This he accomplished in four multivolume works: *The Avenue Story*, *Diana*, *A Horseman Riding By*, and the Swann saga.

Achievement

R. F. Delderfield's greatest achievement is also the source of his enormous popularity in Great Britain and to a large extent in North America too: he presented a vision of a fair-minded, morally superior people evolving peacefully and good-naturedly into a more just and compassionate society than most. That society's leaders, like the heroes and heroines of his sagas, are optimistic, well-meaning egalitarians. They make mistakes. They are sometimes misguided. Villains do take advantage of them from time to time. But inevitably, as there is clearly order in Delderfield's universe, evil is always myopic, and the natural just structure of the universe reasserts itself in a metaphysical manner that seems more Renaissance than modern.

The work of R. F. Delderfield that is most typical of his canon is the three-volume saga *A Horseman Riding* By. That trilogy is also his finest effort. It provides some 1,660 pages of luxurious entertainment while simultaneously teaching a series of historical and political lessons from a centrist, old-fashioned, British Liberal position, which at this writing in the late 1980s has been resuscitated with little success by Britain's new Alliance, the union of the Liberal and Social Democratic parties. *A Horseman Riding By* also succeeds as a family saga. The English reading audience has always enjoyed the story of an extended family enduring, surviving, persevering. Delderfield knew this. He said, "What I really wanted to do was to project the English

way of life in the tradition of Hardy and Galsworthy."[1] To an extent
he did. Delderfield captured some of Galsworthy's sense of the conflict between the fierce, disrupting force of love and the great,
rooted power of family bonding and tradition. In respect to Hardy,
Delderfield partially succeeded as a West Country landscapist, but
shared absolutely none of Hardy's tragic sense of life.

Summation

As a purveyor of quality, classic realistic fiction for popular con-
sumption, R. F. Delderfield has few peers. He skillfully manipulates
the traditional material of the genre: war, death, love affairs, journeys, reversals, and endings that offer a satisfying and generally
acceptable closure. The author's "I" is omnipresent and comforting,
although the texts are written in the conventional third person.
Delderfield's "truths" are those shared by his readers and so their
responses are comfortably passive. They are often moved to tears, but
those tears are more frequently for themselves as the artist's words
skillfully expose and stroke the nerve endings of their own mortality.
Only occasionally are those tears for that kind of suffering that exists
not in the theater, or the family television room, or the library, or
even the heart, but in the streets.

There is, nevertheless, an adjective so often ascribed to R. F.
Delderfield that it cannot and shall not be omitted here. He was
called "beloved." He is a novelist who can provoke a fierce loyalty
created by the audience's belief that they have come to know person-
ally a lovable, compassionate, avuncular author. That kind of adulation was one experienced by Charles Dickens in the nineteenth
century (and it still continues), and by Isaac Bashevis Singer in the
twentieth century.

Delderfield whipped out novels as if Henry James, Marcel Proust,
James Joyce, D. H. Lawrence, and Virginia Woolf had never been
born, as if he did not know that the novel had painstakingly evolved
from mock biography and history to a more self-serving interior
monologue. He did not care. He played his game according to the
old rules, and, critics be damned, he won.

In the twenty-first century the sagas of R. F. Delderfield will
continue to be read as a vision of what it was to be alive and to be

British in the years during and between the reigns of two women: Victoria and Elizabeth II. It is the British story as the British would like it remembered.

Notes and References

Chapter One

1. *Bird's Eye View* (London, 1954), 1; hereafter cited in the text as *BEV*.
2. *Overture for Beginners* (London, 1970), 44; hereafter cited in the text as *OFB*.
3. Barbara A. Bannon, "R. F. Delderfield," *Publishers Weekly* 197, no. 2 (12 January 1970): 29–30.
4. *For My Own Amusement* (New York, 1972), 28; hereafter cited in the text as *FMOA*.
5. *Tales Out of School: An Anthology of West Buckland Reminiscences 1895–1963* (St. Austell, Cornwall, 1963), 14–15; hereafter cited in the text as *TOS*.
6. Dates for plays are of first productions.
7. *For My Own Amusement* (London, 1968), 215; hereafter cited in the text as *FMOA, 1968*.
8. *Nobody Shouted Author* (London, 1951), 140–47; hereafter cited in the text as *NSA*. See also *For My Own Amusement* (1972), 254–56.
9. Webster Schott, "The Delderfield Saga," *New York Times Book Review*, 9 June 1974, 19.
10. Bannon, "R. F. Delderfield," 30.
11. Schott, "Delderfield Saga."
12. Bannon, "R. F. Delderfield," 30.
13. Ibid.

Chapter Two

1. *Spark in Judea* (London, 1953), 80.
2. *This Is My Life* (London, 1944), 27; hereafter cited in the text as *TIML*.
3. *Worm's Eye View* (London, 1948), 69; hereafter cited in the text as *WEV*.
4. *Peace Comes to Peckham* (London, 1948), 102.
5. *The Queen Came By* (London, 1949), 13.
6. *Waggonload o' Monkeys* (London, 1952), 28.
7. *Golden Rain* (London, 1953), 19.
8. *The Offending Hand* (London, 1955), 55.
9. *Where There's a Will* (London, 1954), 54; hereafter cited in the text as *WTAW*.
10. *The Mayerling Affair* (London, 1958), 57–58; hereafter cited in the text as *MA*.

11. *Flashpoint* (London, 1958), 13; hereafter cited in the text as *F*.
12. *Once Aboard the Lugger* (London, 1962), 27.
13. Dates for the one-act plays are publication dates.

Chapter Three

1. *All Over the Town* (London, 1985), 35; hereafter cited in the text as *AOTT*.
2. *Seven Men of Gascony* (London, 1949), 366–67; hereafter cited in the text as *SM*.
3. *Farewell, the Tranquil Mind* (London, 1967), 51–53; hereafter cited in the text as *FTM*.

Chapter Four

1. *The Avenue Story* (London, 1964), vii–viii; hereafter cited in the text as *A*.
2. *Diana* (London, 1984), 11; hereafter cited in the text as *D*.

Chapter Five

1. "The Lure of 'I,' the Tyranny of 'He,' " *Techniques of Novel Writing*, ed. A. S. Burack (Boston, 1973), 96.
2. *Stop at a Winner* (New York, 1978), 52; hereafter cited in the text as *SW*.
3. *The Spring Madness of Mr. Sermon* (London, 1963), 23; hereafter cited in the text as *SM*.
4. *Too Few for Drums* (New York, 1964), 79; hereafter cited in the text as *TFD*.
5. *Cheap Day Return* (London, 1967), 5; hereafter cited in the text *CDR*.
6. *Come Home Charlie and Face Them* (London, 1969), 15; hereafter cited in the text as *CHCFT*.

Chapter Six

1. *Long Summer Day* (London, 1982), 177; hereafter cited in the text as *LSD*.
2. *Post of Honour* (London, 1982), 11; hereafter cited in the text as *PH*.
3. *The Green Gauntlet* (London, 1970), 11; hereafter cited in the text as *GG*.

Chapter Seven

1. "A Qualified Disclaimer," in *To Serve Them All My Days* (New York, 1972).

2. *To Serve Them All My Days* (London, 1972), 621; hereafter cited in the text as *TST*.

3. *God Is an Englishman* (New York, 1970), 686; hereafter cited in the text as *GIE*.

4. Edgar Johnson, *Charles Dickens: His Tragedy and Triumph* (New York, 1952), 509.

5. *Theirs Was the Kingdom* (New York, 1971), 299; hereafter cited in the text as *TWK*.

6. *Give Us This Day* (New York, 1973), 603; hereafter cited in the text as *GUTD*.

Chapter Eight

1. *Napoleon in Love* (New York, 1979), 12; hereafter cited in the text as *NIL*.

2. *The March of the Twenty-Six: Napoleon's Marshals* (London, 1962), 55; hereafter cited in the text as *NM*.

3. *The Golden Millstones: Napoleon's Brothers and Sisters* (London, 1964), 151; hereafter cited in the text as *GM*.

4. *The Retreat from Moscow* (London, 1967), 13; hereafter cited in the text as *RFM*.

5. *Imperial Sunset: The Fall of Napoleon 1813–1814* (New York, 1968), 286; hereafer cited in the text as *IS*.

6. *Under an English Sky* (London, 1964), 11.

7. Ibid., 208.

8. *The Adventures of Ben Gunn* (London, 1956), 9; hereafter cited in the text as *BG*.

Chapter Nine

1. "R. F. Delderfield," in *The Author Speaks: Selected Publishers Weekly Interviews 1967-1976* (New York, 1977), 36.

Selected Bibliography

PRIMARY SOURCES

1. Novels

The Adventures of Ben Gunn. London: Hodder & Stoughton 1956; Indianapolis: Bobbs Merrill, 1957.

All Over the Town. London: Bles, 1947; New York: Simon & Schuster, 1977.

The Avenue Story. London: Hodder & Stoughton, 1964. Published in the U.S. as *The Avenue* (New York: Simon & Schuster, 1969). Originally in two parts: *The Dreaming Suburb* (London: Hodder & Stoughton, 1958) and *The Avenue Goes to War* (London: Hodder & Stoughton, 1958).

Cheap Day Return. London: Hodder & Stoughton, 1967. Published in the U.S. as *Return Journey* (New York: Simon & Schuster, 1974).

Come Home Charlie and Face Them. London: Hodder & Stoughton, 1969. Published in the U.S. as *Charlie Come Home* (New York: Simon & Schuster, 1976).

Farewell, the Tranquil Mind. London: Laurie, 1950. Published in the U.S. as *Farewell the Tranquil* (New York: Dutton, 1950).

Give Us This Day. London: Hodder & Stoughton; New York: Simon & Schuster, 1973.

God Is an Englishman. London: Hodder & Stoughton; New York: Simon & Schuster, 1970.

A Horseman Riding By. London: Hodder & Stoughton, 1966; New York: Simon & Schuster, 1967. Sequel: *The Green Gauntlet* (London: Hodder & Stoughton; New York: Simon & Schuster, 1968).

Seven Men of Gascony. London: Laurie; Indianapolis: Bobbs Merrill, 1949.

The Spring Madness of Mr. Sermon. London: Hodder & Stoughton, 1963. Published in the U.S. as *Mr. Sermon* (New York: Simon & Schuster, 1970).

Stop at a Winner. London: Hodder & Stoughton, 1961; New York: Simon & Schuster, 1978.

Theirs Was the Kingdom. London: Hodder & Stoughton; New York: Simon & Schuster, 1971.

There Was a Fair Maid Dwelling. London: Hodder & Stoughton, 1960. Published in the U.S. as *Diana* (New York: Putnam, 1960). Sequel: *The Unjust Skies* (London: Hodder & Stoughton, 1962). Both volumes in *Diana* (London: Hodder & Stoughton, 1980).

Too Few For Drums. London: Hodder & Stoughton, 1964; New York: Simon & Schuster, 1971.
To Serve Them All My Days. London: Hodder and Stoughton; New York: Simon & Schuster, 1972.

2. Nonfiction

Bird's Eye View. London: Constable, 1954. Autobiograpy.
For My Own Amusement. London: Hodder & Stoughton, 1968; New York: Simon & Schuster, 1972. Latter edition contains 126 more pages and is substantially different. Autobiography.
The Golden Millstones: Napoleon's Brothers and Sisters. London: Weidenfeld & Nicolson, 1964; New York: Harper, 1965.
Imperial Sunset: The Fall of Napoleon 1813–1814. Philadelphia: Chilton, 1968; London: Hodder & Stoughton, 1969.
The March of the Twenty-Six: The Story of Napoleon's Marshals. London: Hodder & Stoughton, 1962. Published in the U.S. as *Napoleon's Marshals* (Philadelphia: Chilton, 1966).
Napoleon in Love. London: Hodder & Stoughton, 1959; Boston: Little Brown, 1960.
Nobody Shouted Author. London: Laurie, 1951. Autobiography.
Overture for Beginners. London: Hodder & Stoughton, 1970. Autobiography.
The Retreat from Moscow. London: Hodder & Stoughton; New York: Atheneum, 1967.
Tales Out of School: An Anthology of West Buckland Reminiscences 1895–1963. St. Austell, Cornwall: H. E. Warne, 1963. Editor.
These Clicks Made History: The Stories of Stanley ("Glorious") Devon, Fleet Street Photographer. Exmouth, Devon: Raleigh Press, 1946.
Under an English Sky. London: Hodder & Stoughton, 1964. Travel.

3. Drama

Absent Lover: A Plantagenet Improbability. London: French, 1953.
All Over the Town. London: French, 1948. Adapted from his novel.
And Then There Were None. London: French, 1954.
The Bride Wore an Opal Ring. London: French, 1952.
Flashpoint. London: French, 1958.
Golden Rain. London: French, 1953.
The Guinea-Pigs. London: Deane, 1954.
Home Is the Hunted. London: French, 1954.
Made to Measure. London: French, 1952.
The Mayerling Affair. London: French, 1958.
Miaow! Miaow! London: French, 1952.
Musical Switch. London: de Wolfe & Stone, 1954.
The Offending Hand. London: Deane, 1955.

The Old Lady at Cheadle. London, Deane, 1952.
Once Aboard a Lugger. London: French, 1962.
The Orchard Walls. London: French, 1954.
Peace Comes to Peckham. London: French, 1948.
The Queen Came By. London: Deane; Boston: Baker, 1949.
The Rounderlay Tradition. London: Deane, 1954.
Sailors Beware. London: Deane, 1950.
Smoke in the Valley. London: French, 1953.
Spark in Judea. Boston: Baker, 1951; London: de Wolfe & Stone, 1953.
Ten till Five. London: de Wolfe & Stone, 1954.
The Testimonial. London: French, 1953.
This Is My Life. London: Fox, 1944. With Basil Thomas.
Uncle's Little Lapse. London: de Wolfe & Stone, 1955.
Waggonload o' Monkeys: Further Adventures of Porter and Taffy. London: Deane, 1952.
Where There's a Will. . . . London: French, 1954.
Wild Mink. London: French, 1962.
Worm's Eye View. London: Sampson Low, 1946; New York: French, 1948.

SECONDARY SOURCES

Bannon, Barbara A. "R. F. Delderfield." *Publishers Weekly*, 12 January 1970, 29–30. Biographical interview. Delderfield outlines plans for Swann saga as at least a tetralogy.
Schott, Webster. "The Delderfield Saga." *New York Times Book Review*, 9 June 1974, 19. Excellent overview and appreciation of Delderfield at the height of his popularity, just shortly after his death.

Index